HEARTLAND EXPRESS

Heartland Express

Journeys by train through New Zealand

Graham Hutchins

Illustrated by Roger McLaren

HarperCollins*Publishers* New Zealand

The author wishes to acknowledge the contributions made by Russell and Julia Young in compiling this book.

First published 1998

HarperCollins*Publishers (New Zealand) Limited*
P.O. Box 1, Auckland

Copyright © Graham Hutchins, 1998

Graham Hutchins asserts the moral right to be identified as the author of this work.

All rights reserved. No part of this publication may be reproduced, stored in a retrieval system or transmitted in any form or by any means, electronic, mechanical, photocopying, recording or otherwise, without the prior written permission of the publishers.

ISBN 1 86950 287 6

Designed and typeset by Egan-Reid Ltd
Cover photograph by James Lawson
Printed by Griffin Press Pty Ltd, South Australia

CONTENTS

Introduction	7
1. Day train through the heartland	11
The Overlander	
2. Coasting on the Coastal	33
The Coastal Pacific	
3. Breakfast at Tuffy's	45
Time out: Christchurch	
4. Stultified by the grandeur	51
The TranzAlpine	
5. Southern exposure	73
The Southerner	
6. On a wing tip and a prayer	87
Time out: Dunedin–Wellington	
7. Way out east	93
The Bay Express	
8. Tunnel vision	103
The Kaimai Express	
9. Into the steamy beyond	117
The Geyserland	
10. Night train	123
The Northerner	
11. Last train to Waiheke	135
Time out: Waiheke Island	

INTRODUCTION

Towards the end of a long, morose winter, it seemed like a good thing to do. Take a train jaunt. 'Around New Zealand in eight days', or 'Around New Zealand in eight trains', alluding to the specific Tranz Scenic long-distance passenger services: the Overlander, Northerner, Kaimai Express, Geyserland, Bay Express, Coastal Pacific, TranzAlpine and Southerner.

Michael Palin had set the pace with his heroic adherence to deadlines while travelling from Kerry to Derry and elsewhere. My original plan was to undertake a New Zealand-sized train marathon, rushing from terminal to junction, outwitting jumbled timetables, jumping the tracks, hitching a ride between connections, catching winks of sleep between rescheduling. But that seemed to be unnecessarily obsessive and strenuous. Besides, the best way to see New Zealand by train is at a pace somewhere between sedate and leisurely.

It was escapism, no doubt about that, but as a confirmed rail buff it had always puzzled me why I hadn't developed a hankering to check out the new, integrated Tranz Scenic services much earlier. Perhaps I figured that New Zealand long-distance passenger services of the 1990s were now the preserve of tourists. Boutique trains that tip-toed through back yards in a fashion totally alien to the rip-snorting steam-hauled expresses of less complicated times.

Trains, planes and automobiles. You take your pick in some ways, although your travel preferences are often contrived by conditioning and environment. To grow up — to wake up — in Te Kuiti in the 1950s was to be bombarded by the sights, sounds, smells and bravura of the railway. For some, the railway formed little more than an aural sounding board, a constant backdrop against which you lived your life. For others, a besottedness set in. I fell into the latter category, carrying the brainstorming memories of trains into reaches where railways didn't go. Writers have eulogised and speculated for years about the appeal of trains. As a writer I retouched base with the rail theme through a series of railway yarns published in 1995. But to seek only sniggers at the expense of the railways seemed totally one-dimensional. In terms of writing about New Zealand railways there was a bigger emotional picture. One that I had neglected for too long.

It used to strike me as being highly significant and slightly scary that, in the old days of the overnight express, 500 perfect strangers could pass through our small town, thereby swelling the population, however temporarily, by 20 per cent, before disappearing into the night. Trains have always been slightly mystical like that.

> The distant hum of expectation.
> The expectation of distance . . .

Waiting for a train still gets the adrenaline flowing. Travelling long-distance is still a commitment, but one you are prepared to make. There's something slightly meaningless about short train journeys, with no time to adjust to the rhythm of the train, the camber of the land and the mood of fellow travellers. So once again I decided to take the train and take what comes. Revisit the old vibes and experience some totally unexpected twists. Trains

INTRODUCTION

can still feel like time capsules, hermetically sealed against the elements and outside forces, hurtling through spheres of influence that remain largely untouched. But some things are new.

On the Tranz Scenic services I expected the matchless scenery, having travelled most routes in earlier years, in various incarnations assembled by good old New Zealand Railways: red, rattling railcar, overnight express, daylight limited down the main trunk line.

I expected the comforts of home associated with New Zealand train travel in the 1990s, having already sampled services run by Tranz Scenic. What I didn't expect was the human contact. The richness of the shared rail experience. Perfect strangers evolved into nodding acquaintances, and finally flowered, as the train threaded its way through the various heartlands, into staunch companions. Tinged with the knowledge that such encounters would inevitably be transitory, a greater level of committment was often apparent. Perhaps it was the freedom inherent in the knowledge that you would never see these people again that eased the interpersonal shackles.

The train goes where other forms of transport fear to tread. Roads tend to hug the contours of the land. From 30,000 feet, it's all just a pretty, mottled pattern, and people are invisible to the jet-borne eye. But the train either ploughs straight through each landscape or takes the high road over viaduct and spiral.

Each Tranz Scenic service had its own appeal and character. The Overlander provided scenic diversity, the Northerner, a unique status as New Zealand's only night train. The Kaimai and Bay Expresses, and the Geyserland, the short-haul North Island trains, appealed for their regional characteristics and the branchline flavour. The Coastal Pacific had its ocean aspect, the TranzAlpine, world famous alpine diversions. The Southerner, the longest-established service, trundling down the oldest railway route in New Zealand, plunged into the deepest south, past the old New Zealand, until we reached the end of the line.

> Bluff or bust?
> There's no bluffing down here.
> It's for real, the weather,
> Five seasons in one day,
> And the night as black as KA coal,
> The wind as wet
> As Stillwater Station on the Midland Line.

The Southener, and Tranz Scenic services, ends its long haul at Invercargill. It's a pity the train could not go on forever, to Bluff and beyond, with the occupants developing a lifestyle of their own. Diesel-drawn nomads in steel capsules, flitting through the heartland well beyond everyday encumbrances.

DAY TRAIN THROUGH THE HEARTLAND: THE OVERLANDER

Overlander comes through here
on its way up north,
Fires up my wanderlust,
for what it's worth.
I hear the hooting whistle blast,
above the rising rain.
I've given all I've got to give,
just wanna take that train.

Somewhat incongruously, I begin my odyssey in the middle of the land-locked Waikato, Te Awamutu to be precise, closest station to my home in the King Country. Incongruously, in that I should ideally be setting out from the terminus — Auckland, City of Sails. But in terms of a somewhat inverted itinerary, I intend doing the Auckland–Te Awamutu segment some weeks after the 'Round the Rest of New Zealand in 8 Days' junket.

The latter will see me and my photographer/researcher, Russell 'Paparazzi' Young of Te Kuiti, travel on the Overlander to Wellington; the Interislander ferry to Picton; the Coastal Pacific from Picton to Christchurch; the TranzAlpine from Christchurch to Greymouth and back; and the Southerner from Christchurch to Invercargill, and back to Dunedin.

We break the habit, and lose a few points in the authenticity stakes, by flying back to Wellington, from where we will catch the Bay Express to Napier. To fill in the gaps and touch base with the remaining Tranz Scenic long-distance services we will, at our leisure and at a later date, take the Kaimai Express from Tauranga to Hamilton, before transferring to the Geyserland, which will ease us back down another of the 'fingerling' lines of the Waikato–Bay of Plenty, to Rotorua. Finally, the night train, the Northerner, will take us north to Auckland.

And then we will take the last leg, complete the cycle in fact, on the Overlander back to our home base in the King Country. We will finish at the beginning, so to speak.

Te Awamutu station is a sterile structure. Mind you, Te Awamutu was never your archetypical Waikato-King Country railway town at any time in its history, not like the T-towns of the real heartland, Te Kuiti, Taumarunui, Taihape.

Down at the station, Te Awamutu, 1997, the peace is profound. No traffic down here, be it road or rail, not while I'm waiting for the Overlander anyway. The rising wind rustles the trees, casting shadows over a nearby sawdust dump. The rustling sounds a bit like an approaching train. By now I am primed by expectation and a certain nervousness. What if the Overlander doesn't stop at Te Awamutu? It's not a prepossessing station. Stuck in the middle of nowhere. Barely a whistlestop. Fairly unwelcoming.

As arrival time draws near, every noise sounds like an incoming train. You sense the steel lines humming. The constant low moan of the nearby dairy factory sounds like an Overlander. At least in the old days of my Te Kuiti association with incoming expresses, there would be an almighty clatter as decelerating trains encountered the Te Kumi rail bridge. Not here though. In fact, I am still harking back to Te Kuiti days when the Overlander, headed by electric engine EF 30065, ghosts quietly towards the station. A friendly greeting from the train manager (they used to call them guards in days when certain sections of the train were indeed like prison wings), a flurry of hand gestures as tickets are forfeited, and the Overlander is gliding smoothly into the green, green, green of home.

Unlike the days when guards probably had to be gruff, there is no one sprawled across my reserved seat. No grunting behemoth snoring like a backwoods chainsaw, sleeping through his station. Of course, this is a daylight service, not the old night express between Auckland and Wellington which, according to your mood, was either a chortling amalgam of light-hearted confusion, full of character and characters, or a wildly swaying swillery, in which thick crockery (and fellow passengers?) chipped teeth, and sleep was abandoned just this side of Taumarunui.

Inside the Overlander the mood is subdued, the passengers intent on taking in the rolling hills and whatever else happens along the way. Otorohanga, gateway to the Waitomo Caves, sees the train ease to a stop and suddenly the platform is awash with tourists and backpackers. In the time it takes to fill two tourist buses to the gunwhales, Otorohanga almost doubles in population. The upgrading of the station buildings and environs is a credit to whoever is responsible for such improvements. The handling of the off-train, on-bus logistics is a credit to train staff and bus drivers, who step into high gear to process the glow-worm seeking hordes.

Between Otorohanga and Te Kuiti a strange uneasiness nags at me. Even before the train begins to brake as it clatters across the Te Kumi rail bridge, things are moving in slow motion. Returning to my home town by train summons up some powerful memories. I recall how welcoming the town used to be in the 1960s when, completing my journey on the 7.30 p.m. express, the street lights flickered like beacons, friendly glow-worms in a familiar valley, set against a towering hill-girt skyline.

Drifting past the old school crossing brings back memories of a not-so-distant past. A plume of diesel smoke coughs into the air, casting my mind back to the steam-drawn Muster Express that terminated at Te Kuiti in 1993. But then I realise the Overlander wouldn't be emitting diesel fumes. We are now electric-hauled. The diesel smoke, pungently nostalgic in its own right, has come from a throbbing big rig waiting at the old school crossing to the north of the town.

I see Te Kuiti's main street, and recall the garb it had worn on that remarkable day in 1993 when the Muster Express and hundreds of people, rural and urban, came to town to participate in the Te Kuiti Muster; a cornucopia of King Country colour and ambience, daubing heartland hues on a dense tapestry of small-town country life. Everyone had a bloody good time, too.

Bagpipers in kilts. Little kids looking up bagpipers' kilts. Confusion reigning as the heavy smoke-drift from KA 942 hauling the Muster Express threw the main street into midday shadow. The steam train smoke of antiquity, the steam of yesteryear blasting from the friendly beast — the magical, fire-breathing dragon.

'This is how it used to be, Jason,' a father recalled to his son, as the express pulled in an hour behind schedule.

'What, late?' the son replied.

'Not just that, boy,' the father explained somewhat testily.

'What, smoky and noisy? Environmentally unfriendly?'

'Stuff the environment. This is like welcoming an old friend.'

Kids eating wild-pork burgers, kids throwing burgers at the skirling pipers. The Overlander slows to a crawl beyond the old King Street crossing where on Muster day Country Will and the Alamos, a country-and-western band, took pride of place to warble and twang their way through obscure cowboy laments like *Chasing you round the house* and *18 cut roses.* Out on the tarseal, a motley amalgam of Christians marched triumphantly past the Lotto outlet, flapping tracts and 'Jesus Saves' banners, singing *Abide with me* above the clip-clop, head-throbbing bass of Country Will and the Alamos. Remember the Alamos?

Smoke from the K 942 continued to belch out and throw a pall over proceedings and visibility. Somewhere in the midst of the melange the first of the returning 'round the hills' marathon runners wheezed their way through the smoke, towards the finish tape just beyond the Pie Cart. A certain amount of jostling ensued as holy rollers, marathon runners, train-spotters and kids lost their bearings in the smoke-filled canyons of Rora Street. The old plodding Clydesdale didn't miss a beat.

The holy rollers got through. A bank manager called Clark won the marathon, and the Muster Express pulled into the platform as if it was still 1962, and 7.30 p.m. Back then, in 1993, the Overlander had passed through Te Kuiti ten minutes ahead of the Muster Express. An old drunk, delighted to learn that a steam train would be returning to

Te Kuiti, re-enacting days when he was just a young drunk, lurched towards the diesel engine.

'Where's the chimney?' the old man asked as the train manager approached the bedraggled figure threatening the motive force of his train.

'They don't need them anymore, sir.'

The inebriate staggered away and by the time K 942 and the Muster Express did arrive, he had flaked behind a hoarding, secure in the knowledge that steam engines had been streamlined to such an extent that smoke was no longer visible to the naked eye.

Everyone was on deck that day, even the Te Kuiti fire brigade, who provided water for the K.

'Why do steam trains need so much water, Dad?' the son asked the father.

'The driver gets very thirsty,' the father replied with a wink.

The Overlander of 1997 glides to a halt at the all-but-deserted Te Kuiti station. The main street goes about its normal Saturday morning business.

Between Te Kuiti and Taumarunui, Russell and I adapt to our new environment. It is a time for quiet cogitation, complimentary lunch and an early Steinlager. Familiar with the landscape, we take the time to get to know the train. The observation car is full of young Americans who are chattering animatedly, particularly as the mountains of the central plateau hove into view. The rest of the train is relaxed and subdued.

Early afternoon and several passengers have nodded off, stupefied by the gentle hum of air-conditioning and a landscape that is more monotonously rugged than stimulatingly handsome. This is the heart of the King Country, the heartland where hard times strike and folks just get on with living. Mangapehi, Waimiha, Ongarue, battered hamlets that have seen better days;

Okahukura, where the inland Taranaki branch-line snakes away over river and highway before plunging into the backblocks. There's nothing much up that line — just 23 tunnels, a clutch of white-collar criminals at remote Ohura prison, and tiny settlements peopled by beneficiaries and families hacking an existence out of country that is even more broken than the main trunk's heartland route.

There's nothing really new about the stretch south of Te Kuiti. In our days of youthful exuberance, we used to take the old mixed-goods train to Taumarunui and back of a Saturday, feeling like liberated, half-men of the world. King Country might be playing Thames Valley in a rep rugby fixture at the Taumarunui Domain, and the mixed goods was a fun way of getting there and back.

South of Te Kuiti, the land closes in. Green turns to rocky grey. The Overlander passes under the Oio overbridge. Nothing terribly remarkable about that, but for the fact that my grandfather used to own the local Oio hotel. Nothing left of the pub now, little left of the town.

The mountains loom, wreathed in snow. The central plateau takes the train higher. By now we have adjourned to the rear of the observation car and Russ begins his photography assignment with a barrage of snaps. The rest of the passengers have become primed as the Raurimu Spiral begins to unwind its secrets. North American accents trumpet the engineering phenomenon. It's obviously a big drawcard. The carriage is now like a noisy classroom with the teacher called away.

The elderly Japanese woman sitting behind us sits quietly amongst the hubbub. At one point she drifts off to sleep and Russ, in worst paparazzi fashion, takes an angled shot of her profile. Russ also tees up a potentially poignant shot of a younger Japanese woman scrawling on a postcard with Ruapehu in the background.

He manages to wedge himself into an unnatural position that would have put anyone else's back out. It is certainly not a Lord Snowdon pose. Just as everything is set for the shot, the train enters a tunnel and the moment is lost.

'What are you guys up to, huh?' The thick-set American seemed friendly enough, but he did want to know. After we had explained our mission he commenced rattling off 'most everything' he knew about Amtrak, the American rail system, executive restructuring and his recreational religion, gridiron, almost as if he were conducting a TV interview. Our burly, bearded travelling companion became known to us as Amtrak Al, although his real name was probably Clint or Charlton.

Meanwhile, Ruapehu was found to be in partial eruption. The cameras whirred. This was the big one. A puff of effusion on cue for the tourists, almost as if tour operators in cahoots with Tranz Scenic had set off a massive gelignite charge just as the Overlander passed to the west.

'Wow. Far out,' a younger son of gridiron bellowed before taking up a camcorder sniping position just this side of the vestibule.

'We came to New Zealand to see an active volcano and hot damn, it is active. Can you believe that?'

Active volcanoes feature prominently on news bulletins in the USA and Europe. To see a snow-girt mountain spewing out something volcanic at the same time has become an imperative on many northern hemisphere travellers' itineraries.

Just north of Taihape the train drifts to an unscheduled stop. The pantograph has come adrift from the power lines and now the driver is dealing with the problem. Thoughts of electrocution surface, and notions of a driverless train. Can anyone drive this rig? Is there a doctor on board? Do we have an electrician? There is a red-headed English marine biologist back in our carriage and a head librarian from Canberra who has been locked in quiet, contemplative conversation with him. Not quiet enough to escape our pricked ears though. Occupationally, all the other passengers are a mystery. One or two look like rocket scientists or computer technology boffins.

One of our companions in the observation car described himself as a change agent. He started out sounding like some sort of bank employee or advanced cashier but ended up being a hirer and firer of staff, in any given business organisation earmarked for restructuring. Burt Spies, a retired plasterer-come-poultry-farmer, and now a part of our discussion group in the observation car, is used to concrete — the real stuff. Not metaphysical concrete thinking. He is having trouble imagining restructuring as something that doesn't involve rejigging and joisting or exchanging cross-beams for parallel girders. It can be confusing. I recalled a blue suit on TV once talking about 'flattening the pyramid'.

'Won't a lot of Egyptians get crushed?' my 12-year-old daughter asked at the time.

'Flattened staff pyramids, restructured management lines.'

It sounded like the work of artisans and tradespeople to Burt Spies, the born-again poultry farmer.

'I'm applying a bit of this restructuring myself,' Burt reckoned.

'Will there be redundancies?' I probed.

'What do you mean?'

'Has your restructuring led to the laying off of staff?' I persisted.

'No. I restructured by knocking hell out of the old storage shed. Levelled the structure in fact.'

'So there will be no lay-offs, Burt?'

'Not unless I change the chook food.'

The engine driver was able to deal to the pantographs and soon we were ghosting down the incline towards Taihape. Amtrak Al made himself better known to us. An open, sometimes garrulous character, he was an old-fashioned rail enthusiast — a nuts and bolts man. He had been big in timetabling for Amtrak in the Chicago region but had decided to cash up and take in as much international train travel as he could. He might have even retired or been laid off. To a fellow enthusiast like myself, it was fascinating listening to Al's accounts of American trains servicing the North-East corridor and of course the greater Chicago area.

'And I mean greater, buddy.'

With Amtrak Al painting verbal pictures of the States and the constant chatter of his younger compatriots, I felt for a time as if we were cutting through Wyoming into Montana. Meanwhile a woman backpacker began bleating like a sheep as the Overlander sent a flock of merinos scattering. It was the same woman who had jumped to her feet as the train stopped in Ohakune, declaring that she 'wanted pizza real bad', a desire apparently triggered by a pizza parlour sign opposite the station.

A group of young English males made whooping sounds when the PA system announced that the old, abandoned Hapuawhena viaduct was now used for bungy jumping in the weekends. Get down! As we crossed the Makatote viaduct, Mt Taranaki became visible to the east, inducing further air punching, not only by young Americans and English, but also by an elderly Japanese man who all but dropped his video camera.

It was easy enough for New Zealanders to feel blasé. It was pretty impressive scenery, but we tend to take such sights for granted. Amtrak Al put the divergent responses in perspective.

'It's not just that the scenery's so god-damn dramatic, you know. It's also the fact that it's changing all the time — spirals, plateaux, active volcanoes, viaducts, waterfalls, however small. Back home you'd have to go five hundred miles to encounter such diversity. Here it is concentrated in fifty miles.'

Then there was the tussock and lahar country, of which only the tussock was showing. Good thing too, I emphasised to Amtrak Al. Those lahars can get nasty.

'What in God's name is a lahar?' Al looked panic-stricken. I think he thought a lahar was some wild, flesh-eating mammal.

I described the unscheduled flow of sulphurous water and debris from the crater lake of a volcano and how these, once they enter watercourses, can be very destructive, particularly if crater lakes subside unexpectedly, releasing murderous volumes of matter. Lahars eat railway bridges, as the one in 1953 did, causing the Tangiwai disaster.

'So this is deepest lahar country.' Al was trying to sound relaxed, but suddenly the playful puffing of Ruapehu signalled a sinister aspect.

'Don't mention Tangiwai,' could have been a Tranz Scenic PR directive. Or perhaps extramural forces were playing a part.

Certainly the carriage fell silent as the Overlander angled past the bleak, regulation khaki army museum and ghetto station at Waiouru after heading due east over the infamous crossing of the Whangaehu River. Tangiwai, the weeping waters, where the tussock was flecked with icing sugar snow, brought memories of a haunted Christmas.

'Prophetic name,' the slightly built man sitting opposite us proffered.

The heartland had suddenly become dour and edgy. The festive air prevailing as we encountered Ohakune, with its American ski resort facade and pulsing pizza signs, had gone.

The train staff were sounding a bit off-colour now too. At some stage we had exchanged a Bob for a Bruce. Bruce was part of the Wellington-based crew. Bob was returning on the northbound Overlander to Auckland. Someone, Bruce probably, reckoned the next round of complimentary coffee couldn't be served because the Auckland team hadn't transferred the appropriate trolleys. A brief glitch, a spot of malaise that didn't cause serious mutiny in the ranks, not as long as Amtrak Al kept shouting the occasional Steinlager.

Approaching Taihape, Russ wanted to know why I sensed that the Dutch family cavorting in the rear of the observation section was in fact Dutch. He figured they were Scandinavian, Estonian even. Attractive in a sub-slavic way, with tingling complexions. Earlier the person we later came to know as the Professor of Pretoria (he really was a professor) had begun an animated foreign language exchange with the blondish mother. The penny dropped, or the rand. Soon the professor introduced himself to us in that distinctive great-white-hunter-drawl. Well, it's more a compression of vowels than an elongation.

One of the first things we talked about, as the tussock lands of the Central Plateau rolled past, was the iron Afrikaner resolve, how it would soon, after their years of angst and relinquishment of power, impact on Springbok rugby and then — then (the professor's cultured voice was tinged humorously with tones of anticipated revenge) we will 'take you aport' — 'you' being the All Blacks, directly, and us, the Kiwi train travellers, indirectly. As All Black fans, we would soon have our noses rubbed in Louis Luyt's fertiliser on the high veldt as South Africans, through rugby, expressed themselves and reasserted their world dominance.

'Are we talking food poisoning?' Russ asked.

'No. Just fertiliser. Louis Luyt's stuff. On the back of that, and him — or someone like him — we'll take you aport.'

The Overlander crashed into a tunnel and Amtrak Al started guffawing, relieved that his beloved gridiron was safe from critical analysis while such rugby aficionados locked horns.

Approaching Taihape, the gumboot capital, the once friendly sounding, laid-back, archetypical, cocooning New Zealand small town, my mind did a back-up. Travel weariness and an overkill of affectation got to me. A certain 90s negativity descended.

There's something vaguely unsettling about the changes to the social landscape. You see it on the highway, the looming big rigs emblazoned with 'Wattie's Foods' and 'Independent Molasses' gunning down the half-crippled Cortinas. Big business running down those with no business being on the roads at all, not if you listen to the farmer sitting behind us.

'Look at those sardine tins jamming up the highway. Shouldn't be allowed on the roads.'

The farmer's pomposity struck a nerve. I could have pointed out to him that 'Wattie's Foods' and milk tankers could perhaps be using rail instead of clogging the highways. But you could tell by his tone of voice, and the set of his lips, that nothing would get through. He had the sort of mouth-set that when called upon to smile for the camera at some golf club reunion would emit a snarl — a wind-induced grimace. Besides, the milk tankers and big rigs were probably carrying the fruits of his labourers.

The presence of the underclass is a disturbing trend in these pockets of the heartland. You see it in the small settlements and half-horse towns, with the knots of unemployed youths gathering, staring vacantly at the passing train. The unkempt back yards and graffiti-stained stations and hoardings, kids sniffing glue in full view of the rail, although hidden from the patrol cars cruising the streets.

You sense the alienation as the farmer continues to snarl and bemoan the effrontery to his smug senses.

Taihape station and a young mother with a cigarette between what look like bloodied lips, slaps her toddler.

'Bloody DPB bludgers,' the farmer snarls. A BMW pulls up at the station and a gaggle of Japanese tourists rush along the platform, as though it's rush hour on the Tokyo underground, nearly sending the bellowing toddler flying as the mother turns her back on the situation. DPBs and BMWs. I guess you're not supposed to notice the disparities.

The young mother is not catching the train, nor does she seem to be waiting for anyone to alight. Is the station just somewhere to go, some place to be? Time out from a desperate domestic situation? Perhaps the train gives her a glimpse of another way of life. From the wrong side of the beaten track.

As the train eases away from the platform, our eyes meet fleetingly. Her vacant stare makes me feel as though we are both acting in TV soap operas — on different channels. Who is watching whom? Vague unsettling feelings become pangs of guilt. The carriage falls silent again. You wonder how other passengers view the situation, particularly fellow New Zealanders.

It's easy enough to look beyond such misery. The train will soon be moving on into lush farmlands and prosperous rural settings. But then you notice the mausoleums, the massive new houses — the monuments to self — perched on hill tops, overlooking the flaking hovels and rusting Valiant hulks. The stretches of another New Zealand you're not supposed to notice.

Travelling through the heartland of the North Island you continue to see the fragmentation of society. You see again the rural highways, the carnage strips where country people die on country roads, and unsuspecting tourists and urban speedsters come to grief. You pine for the once-familiar comforts of mainline train travel. The homogenous masses waiting for trains that stopped everywhere. The red-cheeked rush to refreshment rooms. The friendly steam engines and gruff guards. The predictability of life. And you long for the vignettes beyond the double-glazing that reflected the old egalitarianism.

Are we travelling on a boutique railway, tiptoeing through blighted back yards that are not really there? God knows you can't help noticing the scenic grandeur, pleasant farms and friendly people in comfortable situations, but next time round there'll probably be noses pressed up against the carriage windows. The 'nation with its nose pressed up against the glass', that Don Henley sang about on 'End of the Innocence'. On the same album he sang of the girl who 'looked at me uncomprehendingly, like cows at a passing train'. It was not unlike the pose struck by the young mother at Taihape Station, who had now disappeared into the vastness of the countryside.

'Come on, buddy. You look a bit morose there.' It was Amtrak Al with a spare can of Steinlager. 'Here, get that down you old chap. You're getting a bit wistificall.'

Okay, so the clusters of small-town youths were merely waiting on an assigned corner for the rugby coach to pick them up, right? And the glue sniffers were only into wallpaper paste? And the young mother with the battered toddler? Well, you can't win them all. Can't change anything either.

'You think that's bad, buddy,' Al continued while straining Steinlager through his stubble. 'You wanna travel through the deep south — on the Gulf Breeze say. Makes New Zealand look like the land of milk and honey.'

'More like milk and money, for some,' I muttered.

'Maybe so, fella, maybe so.' Amtrak Al's final statement on the subject was just a verbal clearing of the throat really.

'At least we don't have paupers travelling on the roofs of our trains like in India,' I added.

'Right on, buddy. They'd be fried like crispy duckling. That power up there arcs like crazy.'

He missed the point, but it didn't matter.

'Crispy duckling's a Chinese dish,' Russ suggested.

'You trying to say they don't have ducks in India, fella?'

'Yes and no.'

'Well, that's all right then.'

As we sped between Marton and Fielding this line of repartee, none too witty, and not at all intellectual, was gradually infused with a more coherent line of patter as the focus of the conversation shifted from Amtrak Al to the Professor of Pretoria and inevitably from the US of A to South Africa. Mind you, as the light died behind the foothills of the Tararuas we were still bogged down in crispy foodstuffs, to wit South African biltong and the perpetual rainbow nation barbecue — the braai.

'Who's this guy, Bill Tong?' Al interjected unhelpfully. The professor had been fascinated by the variety of sheep breeds dotting the landscape of the Rangitikei region.

'They'd go well on the braai.'

'They'd go well on the range back home,' Al announced.

'They'd go well on the electric range right here — and do, I might add,' Russ contributed.

I mumbled something about going well on the Range Rover, for those who could afford them, casting a disdainful glance back at the milk-moneyed farmer who was now knocking back scotch from a series of miniature bottles. He gave me a wink — or was that a facial tic — and belched. The train blasted into a tunnel and the belch seemed to echo.

Marton Junction, and just about everyone on the platform is wearing gumboots.

'I'll tell you this,' Amtrak Al announced. 'New Zealand can get too damn agricultural at times. Know what I mean?'

'What do you mean?' Travel fatigue was catching up with Russ too.

'Well, they've got a town called Bulls, right? You got one called Sheep, huh?'

'They eat a lot of mutton in Marton. Drink a lot of milk too.'

'Exactly. It's like taking god-damn coals to Newcastle.'

'A bit like taking bulls to Bulls.'

'Bullshit.'

We returned to the observation car as the last rays of the

filtered sun receded down the track. Palmerston North station, 5.30 p.m. Darkness descends rapidly.

Memories wash over me. Years before when the old line used to bisect the inner-city square, I had caught the railcar to get to Massey University. On the railcar I encountered a middle-aged woman who lived in Palmerston North, a fellow writer of sorts. She had had a short story published in some periodical. I was working towards that end but couldn't get past the unrealisable dream of becoming the King Country's answer to James K. Baxter. We had a few notes to compare. After much prodding, I burbled a bit of blank verse south of somewhere. She seemed impressed. Or simply unembarrassed. Her insights and deep wells of sadness overwhelmed me. In my naivete, I thought that was what real writers were like. At the time I was reading a lot of an American poet called Robert Lowell who, at his own admission, used to check himself into a mental institution every now and then, when the saddening business of composing his bone-scraping verse got the better of him. Poets — and writers, *per se* — were sad souls, obviously.

It never occurred to me that the woman could be sad for other reasons. At her suburban home in Palmerston North, permeated by the sound of passing trains, she introduced me to her two young sons. Sympathy cards gathered dust on the mantelpiece. Food encrusted plates lay strewn on the kitchen table. The woman's husband had been killed in a car accident two months previously.

I wonder if she's out there somewhere, burbling blank verse.

The conversation in the observation car swirls as the lights of Levin and Otaki twinkle. The exhilaration of the day's journey, and my moments of introspection, are transcended as the Professor, Amtrak Al and Russ and I become drawn into a verbal tussle ranging from rugby, through the rail system of the Chicago area and north-east corridor (not including the State of Maine), all the way to states of inner peace and related ephemera. Some Americans can still talk your ear off, but it's refreshing to be able to report that New Zealanders of the 1990s are now far more aggressive listeners. Russ, something of a student of philosophy, posed a few mind-benders. The professor went along with him. I chucked in the odd oblique one-liner, while Amtrak Al provided even more compendious detail of the upgraded Metroliner service running between Boston, New York and Washington — but not the State of Maine.

'The Springboks will take the All Blacks aport at Eden Pork,' the professor ventured, just south of Paraparaumu.

'The Metroliner's one hell of a train, buddy,' Al maintained.

'The All Blacks will actually prevail at Eden Park,' I ventured, whereupon Amtrak Al whacked me on the back with such force that I was deflected from making a point that might have added weight to my supposition.

'Right on, buddy. But gridiron's all the go, you know.'

The final stretch down the moonlit Kapiti Coast didn't take as long as it usually does. Wellington will be soon upon us. The Overlander is all but spent.

It seems as if we've passed through several time zones, spiralled and inclined across two continents. Amtrak Al and the Professor from Pretoria are like blood brothers now. Funny thing about trains. Because you know you'll probably never see fellow passengers again, a feeling of real freedom of expression develops. I guess the professor could go skulking back to Pretoria, the capital of the Rainbow Nation, and pot us for saying salacious thing about the South African government. Amtrak Al could do the same and whisper in Bill Clinton's ear — or Hillary's. But you know it's not like that.

We have passed through several New Zealands. The milk-

and-money reaches of the Waikato; the dense heartland with its prisons and army strongholds, but also its majestic mountains and deepening rivers running somewhere down there in the bush-clad ravines, beneath the vertiginous viaducts.

Russ, doubling as facilitator, has teed up digs in the capital. Mind you, after rubbing shoulders with our worldly travel companions, Wellington will be a breeze — or a southerly. Amtrak Al turns into a bit of a Waldorf Saladeer when he discovers there is no night service to Napier.

'What sort of railroad is this, huh?'

Our Japanese fellow traveller seems happier now though, in fact there is a dramatic transformation. One of the young American women has drawn her out into a lively conversation that shows the other side of inscrutability — spontaneous laughter. The Japanese woman reveals with each chuckle a mouthful of gold ingot fillings, enough to make you wonder if her reason for not smiling a lot is a self-preserving mechanism to thwart smash and grabbers and gold-diggers.

As the last miles recede, the ramblings of Amtrak Al, the professor, Russ and I have shifted somewhere to a discussion about New Zealand trains of the future. They will be, apparently, like little *Titanics*, with just about every conceivable convenience including in-train videos and music channels, on-board barbers, a creche and a club-car with resident lounge lizard.

'They've already got those in Australia. Lounge lizards of Oz.' I think Russ contributed that.

'A club-car with a guitar band as well as a cocktail pianist.'

'A counsellor for those passengers with travel fatigue, train-lag, homesickness.'

'Pizza addiction.'

'Change agents to remind us of the need to constantly be aware of the need for change.'

'Prostitutes.'

'Tarot card readers.'

'In-house priests. On-board taxidermists.'

'Settle down, huh?'

While this free-floating tirade waxed and waned, as the suburban lights of Paremata spread to the water's edge, the PA announcer kept interrupting our flow with staggered announcements relating to off-loading, on-training, de-training. It was as if a hidden microphone in the observation car was being monitored by the keepers of the train, who, perhaps concerned that our brain-storming could threaten the internal peace and security of the Overlander, were trying to fragment our flow of ideas. Perhaps we were under constant observation. Perhaps that's why they call it the observation car.

'This here Wellington's supposed to be windy, right?' Amtrak Al had already donned his bomber jacket.

'It varies,' I advised as the Overlander glided to a halt, past the expectant faces of waiting platform throngers.

After we had made it outside on to the crowded platform, it was obvious that the weather lacked atmospheric boisterousness. At least down here at the station where swirling passengers in a state of disembarkation created something of a draught of their own.

'This Wellington's no sweat,' Al reckoned. 'They've got worse winds in Wyoming, you know. Frisco's brisk too.'

Amtrak Al led the charge towards the buses and taxis, through the echoing canyons of Wellington station and out into the starry night. He was in the process of taking his bomber jacket off when the first of the southerly blasts struck. He was lucky to hold on to the jacket. The wind, funnelling down Featherston Street, parted his swept-back hair.

The beginnings of a southerly storm were brewing.

COASTING ON THE COASTAL
THE COASTAL PACIFIC

These days a stretch of virgin track is a rarity. In the days of my first railway awakening, in the late 1960s and early 1970s, there was virgin track aplenty. There were lines along which I had never travelled before, along which I felt I had to travel before surviving NZ Rail passenger services were curtailed or the tracks ripped up.

In a few fast months of these services' existence I managed to get from Wellington all the way up to Gisborne via the Wairarapa and Hawke's Bay lines; from Wellington up the other coast to New Plymouth; Stratford to Taumarunui on the SOL, one of NZ Rail's best kept secrets (it has retained this status into the 1990s), Auckland to Opua, and of course the South Island lines: Blenheim to Christchurch, Christchurch to Greymouth. (I actually travelled further down the West Coast to Hokitika, assuming that was the end of the line. The railway promptly went one better — several miles south to the town of Ross.) I journeyed from Christchurch to Invercargill, and the jewel of them all, Alexandra to Dunedin down the old Central Otago line. Even as I travelled, I could sense things closing in — or down. On some stretches I was the only passenger, on others token trains survived in days when certain 'social services' were carried by sentimental governments of the day.

As the Coastal Pacific of 1997 pulled out of Picton station, it was again possible for me to claim that I had never before been on this stretch of track, at least not from Picton to Blenheim. No one else seemed to consider such an event remarkable. In my pantheon of rare treasures, such an experience was almost as epochal as hearing a lost Beatles song.

My senses reeled. Everything became diamond bright: Picton station with its in-house restaurant seemingly far too close to the line — you could see right into diners' shrimp cocktails. An old converted carriage at right angles to the platform served an unknown purpose. Was it a craft shop, a creche, a backpackers' doss house?

The three diesels at the head of the train chuffed purposefully as we began climbing out of the town precincts, until we reached a place with the American-sounding name of Elevation. Very apt too, although it wasn't exactly nose-bleed country.

'No smoking is allowed on this service,' the PA system advised as we continued climbing through gorse-girt cuttings. Someone behind us latched on to the 'smoking is allowed' part of the announcement and began fumbling furiously for her packet of fags. The 'No' word had not registered. Perhaps 'Smoking is not allowed' would have been a better phrase to coin.

The Coastal Pacific sped across the Wairau Plains, seedbed for some of New Zealand's finest wines, before pulling into Blenheim, a burgeoning provincial centre of twenty thousand, spawned, or perhaps reborn, from viticulture dollars. Highest sunshine hours in New Zealand are enjoyed here and to emphasise the point, the sun suddenly broke through the low cloud. And yet Cloudy Bay was just down the road. Whoever named the place must have done so on one of the few days the sun didn't shine. These days if the sun disappears there is always a refreshing chardonnay or two to elevate the mood.

Now we are heading for the coast, curving out over rolling country that looked scorched even in winter, yellowing in this rain-barren corner of the South Island. The track angled back through a horseshoe curve and after negotiating a steep cutting that looked like a large slice out of a coffee cake, the Pacific Ocean came into view. The cutting is a unique piece of railway engineering remembered starkly from my first trip on this line thirty years earlier when we were propelled by a coughing Vulcan railcar, complete with thin-lipped guard and knitting nanas returning home to sensible-sounding towns like Seddon and Ward.

Today the Coastal Pacific edges sleekly out towards the coast with Clifford Bay, the new designated ferry terminal site, glistening beyond the brown hills. An idea awaiting hatching. Lives soon to be changed. A shorter Coastal Pacific route. And what will happen to the withered rail arm from Clifford Bay to Picton? Will it become the wine-taster's rail excursion stamping ground with round trips run for the benefit of the bubbly generation, the coiffured flauntists in wearable art? And maybe a string quartet in the club car.

The Dashwood Pass is breached and words from an obscure railway ditty return:

> They used to mumble threats in '51.
> Now they've got jumbo jets that beat the gun.
> Dashing over Dashwood.
> This rattlesnaking Vulcan's on the run.

We cross, in time, the Awatere road-rail bridge (or rail-road, depending on your preference and priorities). Either way, it's a rarity. It may be the last such dual-purpose transport bridge on the Tranz Scenic network, although I think there's one down Hokitika way. Not that Tranz Scenic go that far south down the

West Coast. Pity. Perhaps the powers-that-be should consider a train called the Westlander from Hokitika via Greymouth and Westport up to Seddonville — if the line still goes that far north. The existence of the upgraded line from Stillwater to the coal mines of Ngakawau, the one that serves the link via the Midland line to the waiting coal freighters at Lyttelton, would significantly reduce the amount of track requiring improvement to accommodate such a service. The Westlander could have a distinctly Westland flavour. Greenstone green livery, coal black engine. Whitebait fritters in the buffet. Monteith's on tap. It could provide a link between the scenic wonderland of Fiordland and the largely untapped tourist potential of North Westland. It could offer backpackers and other hardy souls access to the Heaphy Track. And time for a Farewell Spit...

I am jolted from my daydreams as the Coastal Pacific shudders to a stop at Seddon. We wait here for a good five minutes while the signals change, during which time the PA system advises us that the town Seddon was named after Richard Seddon, former prime minister of New Zealand.

Beyond Seddon one or two passengers begin stretching their legs. For an hour or so the whole train has been in a slightly hungover state. There have been some rough ferry crossings and late nights. A young backpacker in front of us is contorted in the deep sleep of the adolescent, catching up on something. Lake Grassmere and its massive salt deposits materialise, giving rise to a certain amount of speculation.

'Is that where they breed the crayfish, buddy?' It was Amtrak Al in the process of reacquaintance. He looked shot.

'We had one hell of a crossing. Didn't get our heads down until five this morning. Wow. Look at the size of those god-damn galoons.' Al was referring to the massive salt lagoons of the Grassmere complex where a combination of contained seawater and high sunshine hours hastens the evaporation process that produces salt by the tonne. Or by the galore, as Russ harkened back to another malapropism attributed to a mate who used to work in the bakery.

Al, we had already noticed, was inclined to bungle the odd word.

'Look at all that salt. Gives you a connery just looking at it.' The late night and early Steinlager were making their mark. A conveyor belt, part of the salt-stacking apparatus, caused Al some concern. Something of a health and safety expert, he could perceive a weak link in the chain.

'Hey. A man could get injured in the back of that conveyor.'

'A wound in the salt,' Russ coined cleverly.

'You mean salt in the wound, fella,' Al replied, playfully punching Russ on the arm, sending beer spraying across the window. It was no match for the sea spray lashing the outside of the double-glazing. The southerly was ferocious now, the Pacific anything but pacific.

After a while you just conceded to the elements. Despite the stimulating company and riveting conversations, the scenery of the Kaikoura coast sucked you in. Between Wharanui and Hapuku the haze above the skyline hovered, ranging through the spectrum from muted pastels to blazing orange, off-greys and half-blues. Aquamarine sky, varicose horizon.

On a seafront clearing a brace of heavy horses passed water in the wind, as tussock was blown horizontal like slickered hair on a balding pate. You could feel the Coastal Pacific buffet as the southerly howled. Off to the right of the train the Kaikoura Ranges — Seaward and Inland — stood oblivious to man-made intrusions like rail and road. Turned a blind eye to the hurricane, if that's what it was to become, and reports fluctuated as wildly as the Pacific breakers.

Just south of Clarence the wind eased and the sea flattened somewhat. Nowhere near the millpond that gently lapped the coast during my first trip along this sliver nearly thirty years earlier. On that occasion it was the old Vulcan railcar that bucked and undulated, eventually giving up the ghost as a piston blew at Goose Bay. As the wind eases, a patch of blue sky clears. A vapour trail hangs in the sky, above the southerly, one would suspect.

At one point there appear to be four tunnels as the land all but disappears into the sea. Two are road tunnels, one rail and one, out where the black rocks dominate the beach, could be for seals. There are over twenty tunnels along the Coastal Pacific route — perhaps there should be more. At Mangamaunu the train appears to be travelling along the beach as a wall of sea spray smashes against the carriage windows.

As the Coastal Pacific winds its way south, PA announcements keep us up to the mark in terms of historical and geographical line-side features. We also learn the train is running seven minutes late, but that the time will be made up when we hit the straight stretches north of Christchurch. We are also alerted to the fact that trainspotters are a common feature in the isolated settlements wedged between land and sea. Harry of Hapuku is one such character for whom the passing of the Coastal Pacific has become a fullstop — or question-mark — in his day. Certainly a constant in his life. If that's the Coastal Pacific, it must be time to put the dinner on.

Off to the right we notice Harry waving to the train with one hand while holding up a broad-faced clock with the other. It is Harry's way of telling us that the train is running late. On cue, the PA fills us in.

'And there's Harry waving his clock at the train.' The word 'clock' is muffled by momentary static. 'Clock' doesn't sound like 'clock.' Behind us, two women, detecting the gaffe, laugh like barking seals. It is time to restretch the legs.

The 1960s were revisited when I made a significant discovery. At the head of the train, carriage U in fact, a group of noisy revellers were pitching in. Car U was half buffet and half discount seating, certainly enough to accommodate a goodly portion of the population of Geraldine. A Sunday elevenses session in a Blenheim hotel had spilled over into carriage U where the rip-roaring, snorting celebration continued. What they were celebrating was hard to determine. It probably wasn't important. More than likely some end of season rugby junket with everyone drinking too much Speights in too narrow a timeframe, in too confined a space. It was interesting to see such 1960s behaviour on what was very much a 1990s service.

One beer-stained apparition in conflicting garb — league jersey, cricket cap and thigh waders that suggested an involvement in fly-fishing— volunteered a certain amount of information.

'We won mate,' he yelled at me as the train angled sharply around a bend, throwing him momentarily off balance as he straddled the aisle. In horrible slow motion he capsized sideways across a table, sending cans rattling. A great cheer arose from the rest of the carriage. A woman, bloodshot and shirty, confronted me.

'You meant to do that, mate,' she claimed.

'Settle down, Adele,' the man sitting next to her slurred. 'It was just an accident. He didn't touch Terry.'

Terry, disentangling himself from the jostling legs beneath the table, came up grinning. The woman Adele, slightly more than none the worse for Speights, stood her ground.

'What's the password, mate?' she threatened.

'Toilet,' I replied, pointing hopefully at the illuminated sign at the end of carriage U.

'You'll have to do better than that.'

'Please,' I pleaded.

'Look, mate. I've been on this bloody train for two hours and I'm craving two things.'

Why, that's one craving every hour, I thought to myself.

'If you can tell me what I'm craving, I'll let you past.'

'Sandwiches?' I suggested reasonably, knowing that the occupants of the discount seats in carriage U were not entitled to complimentary afternoon tea.

'Sex, mate. She's craving sex,' Terry guffawed from his re-anchored position next to the servery. The woman blushed in an old-fashioned South Island way and I tried to enter into the spirit of the occasion, tried to hide my diffidence by laughing loudly so that everyone would hear.

'Nicotine. That's what it is. I'm not allowed to smoke on this bloody train.'

I suggested that, as we were pulling into Kaikoura, there might be time for a puff or two, to enable some sort of fix. She smiled, punched my arm, and went diving for her handbag.

By now Terry — or Trevor — had cranked up his guitar and a ribald version of 'Down by the Riverside' was taking some of the light-hearted heat out of the situation. By the time the train eased off towards the crayfish capital, the way was clear and I walked purposefully towards the vestibule. I never did find out what the second craving was. Perhaps it was crayfish — or two cigarettes.

As we edged closer to Kaikoura, the open sea was scanned for whales and seals. And dolphins. What may have been a family of seals sat stoically on the rocks. But then again, they could have been small rocks on bigger rocks. The misty rain was driving in again. Evidence of crayfish sprang up beside the track. Vendors' caravans and lean-tos advertised 'Nin's Bin Crays' and 'Gay's Crays', and one remarkable sign boasted snacks like 'Cheese and Union sandwiches', and a German variation, 'Hamburghurs'. Another where the wind had sheered off vital information offered 'Toasted Sand'. But the most bizarre of them was man-made: 'Dognuts' were available at one line-side eatery.

A tunnel portal carried the message 'Jesus is dead', but Kaikoura was alive and crawling with crays.

'Remember the Kray twins?'

'It's a wonder Jim Henson of the Muppets didn't invent a couple of characters called the Cray twins — crayfish with mean streaks. Attitude.'

Kaikoura Station bustled with backpackers. The crayfish theme was adhered to in the station's colour scheme: live crayfish green with red, cooked crayfish edgings. Half of carriage U's occupants were on the platform puffing fags. Their collective blue exhaust rose momentarily before being dashed north by the freshening wind.

As we eased out of Kaikoura, arcing over the main thoroughfare with its Seal Museum signs and Whale Emporiums, the revellers in carriage U had settled down somewhat. 'The green

green grass of home', sung in a wistful monotone, acted as a subduing agent.

Back in my seat, I tried to convey to Russ that the past lives on NZ Rail, once famous for the traditional gut-busting, homeward-bound booze-up after the big, and not so big, game, was still in evidence. I told him about carriage U.

'You must be joking,' he chortled. 'This is the Coastal Pacific, a genteel means of propulsion from A to B.' He even suggested that such a festive happening might have been orchestrated by Tranz Scenic as a tourist attraction. A blast from the past, a bit like a fabricated cowboy shoot-out at Shantytown.

Of course, by the time he inspected the scene the sting had gone out of the celebration. Russ accused me of having floundered in some time-warp summoned up by wishful thinking and travel fatigue. I knew what I saw. Memories of 'Hard Knocks', an old rail ballad, arose.

> Scrambled on the seven-thirty,
> Latrines were filthy, the fitments dirty.
> The beer flowed down carriage E, non-smoking.
> Crawled towards a vacant box,
> among the students from the University of Hard Knocks.
> The beer flowed three feet deep, no joking.

The mesmeric roar of trains. The soporific swish and sway. The flitting images of half-light as refractions and reflections dance off the double-glazing. Somewhere in the reflected faces you see images of loved ones. Lost souls. People can look lonely in the half-light. Miles from home. Travel weariness setting in. A sea of nameless faces cocooned in vocal silence listening to the all-pervading roar of the train. The bonhomie of the day's trip dissolves as our destination approaches. Travellers slowly begin to gather up belongings and make ready. Anxiety etches faces as they contemplate a late arrival and no one to meet them at the station.

As a kid, I used to feel sorry for alighting passengers, those with no one waiting on the platform for them. The great gales of greeting sounds from loved ones and family washed over and beyond them. Their lot was a slow trudge into the night, wherever lone travellers went — after the train.

If only the train could go on forever. An English girl with cancer, who we had encountered all too briefly as the Coastal Pacific passed through the northern suburbs of Christchurch, gathered up her hand luggage and eased towards the door.

'Have a good life,' she yelled back at us. ('I guess I'll just keep travelling until I can travel no more.') Her earlier words repeated like the refrain of a confessional rock ballad from the 1970s. She would doubtless put down in some backpackers' hostel, surrounded by people yet quite alone. She'd already said goodbye to family and friends in Britain. They honoured her wish to see the world before she died. They did not deny her the right to do so on her own, for herself. She'd always been a loner. Now, just this side of twenty, in that emotional watershed between youth and adulthood, she had retreated as much into herself as she had to the other side of the world.

And yet there was a steely glint in her eye. She smiled a lot, even when our jokes weren't funny. You wanted to travel with her to the end of the earth, to make sure she made it to the last of the backpackers' hostels. But the shield around her seemed impenetrable, even if you'd been silly enough to try to get closer.

'You can write about me in your book, if you like,' she mentioned casually as we hove to in the aisle. I gave a hopeful thumbs up sign. It seemed a pathetic gesture. I couldn't think of anything to say. I could have promised to send her a copy, but knowing the time it takes to assemble a book, would she still be travelling? There was something terribly determined in those eyes though. Something that seemed to make a mockery of the transfusion scars on her wrists.

She walked off into the night, beyond the garish station lights. I watched her disappear into the shadows as sirens began wailing in the city streets.

'Missed your chance there, old chap,' Amtrak Al boomed as he slapped me on the back.

'You missed the point,' I thought, as the American continued to don his pseudo-British accent.

'We'll see you on the TranzAlpine, old boy, old chap.'

The lights of Christchurch beckoned. We stood on the windswept platform feeling cold and abandoned. During the course of our trip from Picton we had not only been privileged to see some of the most breathtaking scenery in the world, but we had also entered into some special interpersonal orbits, experiencing the human factor that can really only unravel on long-distance trains. Buses sway and you're not even allowed to converse with the driver. Planes are all about A to B convenience and speed. And the motor car is just a cone of silence on wheels, a vessel to express your right to go it alone.

If only the train could go on forever.

BREAKFAST AT TUFFY'S
TIME OUT —
CHRISTCHURCH

Breakfast at the hotel had its moments. At about 8.30 a.m. I wandered into the shabby 1950s dining room which was deserted, save for a handful of hotel staff. One middle-aged man in a brown cardigan and red and black tie operated as mine host/waiter. It was like walking through the portals of the Lyttelton tunnel in steam days. I'd just missed the breakfast sitting. The earlier breakfasters must have all been heavy smokers if the hovering, blue smoke cloud and crushed butts in ashtrays and porridge plates were anything to go by.

'Morning, Sir. You've just missed the breakfast rush.' The man in the brown cardigan was friendly enough.

'Haven't just missed the breakfast too, have I?' One of the kitchen staff was boarding up the servery.

'You might be lucky. If you go through and talk to Tuffy the cook, he might whip you up something.'

The kitchen was an old-world, begrimed edifice, reeking of an uneasy combination of stale bacon fat and disinfectant. Tuffy the cook, a hulking man with a black eye, was scraping fat off a hot plate and slapping it into a bucket.

'Can you do bacon and eggs?' I asked.

'Can do,' he grunted between slaps of fat.

HEARTLAND EXPRESS

Back in the dining room the smoke had cleared and I chose a table next to the window. Not that that was any sort of advantage. The window was painted over with brown paint. The only thing visible, if you craned your neck, was a series of extractor fans that obviously earned their keep. Sundry crashes and curses filtered through from the kitchen.

Another guest wandered in supported by a pair of crutches.

'What happened to you, Ray?' the brown cardigan asked, while thumping a tardy tea urn.

'Broke my leg at the league.'

'Anyone would think you were playing.'

'Bloody terraces had ice on them.'

'ACC eh, Ray?'

'Guess so. Is the cook still in?'

'Just.'

'Is he talking?'

'I can't hear anything. He's certainly not singing.'

Ray with the crutches eased himself into the kitchen. A loud, brief exchange of unpleasantries ensued. Eventually I was presented with six bucks worth of bacon and eggs and several complimentary cups of coffee. Outside, beyond the brown windows, the Canterbury weather packed up. We had been planning on taking the TranzAlpine this morning but opted instead for a rest day. The murmurings of the southerly storm we had encountered near Kaikoura were now fully fledged, and the rail run up to Arthur's Pass would have been miserable and misty. The same storm was to cause the cancellation of several Interislander crossings.

Fortified by a large breakfast and lashing of thermal vests, I braved the city streets. As part of my travelling strategy, plenty of street walking to shake off travel lethargy had been programmed into the itinerary. Just because Christchurch was experiencing one-degree temperatures, it didn't seem a valid reason for confining myself to a hotel room. Mind you, the air was crisp and the zephyrs keen as I wandered around the inner city. For two hours I endured the elements. The wind certainly buffeted, but this was balanced by an accumulation of CMS — Constant Motion Syndrome. After 48 hours of being thrown around in the altered gravity of the

Overlander and Coastal Pacific, not to mention the welling surges of the Interislander, the blustery southerly in Cathedral Square was neither here nor there.

I made it all the way around to Moorhouse Avenue, site of the old brick railway station, before heading back down Colombo Street. Our hotel was only a couple of hundred metres from the old station. What an advantage that would have been if Addington station had not become the new departure terminal.

Pleasantly surprised at my efforts to withstand the southerlies, I dropped into a café which rather ambitiously still had a few seats and tables set up on the pavement. Several plastic chairs had been dumped by the wind into the gutter. The café was warm and welcoming, though. A young man in Hawaiian shirt sleeves greeted me enthusiastically.

'Not so hot outside, mate,' he began, flashing his forearms.

My mind was cast back to the freezing night before, when the young female receptionist at the hotel presented a bare midriff as we signed the register. Young blood, eh? Fashion slaves?

'Feel the earthquake?' The bare forearms continued, while activating the espresso machine, inducing a sound that was not unlike that of a small elephant in a state of strangulation.

I began to explain that because of the buffeting wind and my CMS, an earthquake registering less than six on the Richter scale would probably go undetected. It was then that I discovered my face muscles, lips and tongue had been rendered rigid by the cold. After making a series of burbling noises, Captain Espresso probably inclined to the view that I was a bit simple and turned his attention elsewhere.

The coffee was hot and steamy. I soaked my face in the mocha vapour to help thaw my cheek muscles.

Back in the hotel room, it was time to expand aspects of our journey so far, while the storm continued to lash and dump.

Later in the day we ducked down to McDonald's for a quick burger. If anything, the wind felt colder. The crowd in McDonald's looked as though they were attending a Sherpas' conference — there were certainly no Hawaiian shirt sleeves or bare midriffs. Even the plastic smiles of 'Tracey' and 'Jason' behind the counter looked frozen. Fingers fused by the cold malfunctioned. Someone dropped their tray in the path of a swathe of Japanese tourists who, preoccupied with their giggling, ground chips into the tile floor.

'The chips are down,' Russ mumbled around a mouthful of McBurger.

Another tourist, disorientated by the cold, appeared to post a handful of postcards in the 'tray return' slot.

We returned to our hotel room and began thawing out all over again. Hopefully the worst of the storm might have dissipated by the time we assembled at Addington station the following morning.

STULTIFIED BY THE GRANDEUR (THE EIGHTH WONDER) THE TRANZALPINE

The TranzAlpine is one hell of a train, world famous in fact, and justifiably so. In the course of a day's travel from Christchurch to Greymouth and back, you pass through an encapsulation of scenic grandeur that is immediately accessible and constantly changing. It's like enjoying a sneak preview of a Fellini movie. In retrospect, it's probably more Steven Spielberg. You imagine that if Spielberg wanted to make a blockbusting opus that called for a scenic backdrop of unmitigated grandeur, he would either resort to graphically enhanced special effects or film his movie against a landscape made accessible by the Midland line along which the TranzAlpine wends its way.

The richness of the country is overwhelming. Sometimes you feel as if you can't take it all in at once. Then you realise that you don't necessarily have to. The knowledge that the TranzAlpine returns along the same tracks, past the same sights for sore eyes, enables you to switch off at times when overload threatens your sensory receptors.

It all begins innocently enough. Addington station, Christchurch, 8-something a.m. Seven carriages, most of them surprisingly full. Such generous patronage could be put down to a block booking. That's what it must be. The total complement of a local rest-home had probably chosen the same day to take the train.

This was not the case. The TranzAlpine was always heavily patronised.

'Make no mistake. It's a biggy,' the American tourist sitting across from us volunteered. He was referring to the reputation of the TranzAlpine and how significant it had become, not just as a rail enthusiast's 'must-see', but as a genuine tourist attraction in its own right.

'It's kinda like going through the Canadian Rockies in a quarter of the time.'

We struck a chord on that one. Several years earlier I too had travelled from Vancouver in British Columbia to Calgary, Alberta, and yes, while the alpine scenery of the Canadian Rockies was impressive, it tended to go on a bit too long.

'Is it anything like the Oslo to Bergen in Norway?' I asked.

'Haven't done that one buddy, but I do know that it's nothing like the San Antonio de Los Cobres to Socompa trip through the Andes.'

About a quarter of a mile after pulling out of Addington the train lurched to a halt.

'We are stopping here to pick up the driver,' the PA system advised.

Had he fallen over? Too much Speights on his porridge? No, it was simply a matter of the driver, in a totally sober state, joining the train beyond the shunting yards. So who had been driving the train up to this point? Amtrak Al or some other enthusiast with a desire for hands-on involvement? A local Christchurch identity like the Wizard, or Grizz Wyllie?

Soon we were gathering speed through the southern suburbs of Christchurch and the matter was not pursued. Other issues became pressing. How close would we run to Hoon Hay, the suburb with the most uncomplimentary of names? Twenty years earlier the name Hoon Hay would strike you as being vaguely amusing, representing perhaps some Scottish stronghold in a very English area of population transplantation. However, with the emergence of hoons, the young male drivers of beat-up or souped-up earlier-model cars, Hoon Hay had taken on a new significance. A bit like the name Trevor developing humorous overtones simply because Fred Dagg, the Kiwi icon, had seven sons all named Trevor.

Hoon Hay was not in the picture, in terms of the southern rail route out of Christchurch. It lay some distance to the west, and we were informed by an eavesdropping Fendaltonian that it contained fewer hoons than New Brighton — or Te Kuiti.

As we rattled through the industrial suburbs, the outline of fellow passengers came into focus. Opposite us, sharing the central table, was a well-dressed, middle-aged woman and her companion, an older man with both arms in a sling. Had he been to the league too? Plaster casts extended from both shoulders to both sets of fingers. At first we thought he was wearing a strait-jacket but the woman soon explained that her husband had been in a car accident, and a trip on the TranzAlpine was a therapeutic means of taking his mind off two broken arms and a hairline skull fracture.

Can anything take your mind off a hairline skull fracture, I pondered? Wasn't it a bit like taking a stiff walk to get some feeling back into a broken leg? The man just stared out the window at the Canterbury Plains, and soon we pulled into Rolleston, the junction station. Beyond this point, we would be committed to the Midland line, that amazing engineering feat that managed to cleave the Alps and expose the West Coast.

It was time for morning tea — club sandwiches with lashings of hot coffee. As the train gathered speed towards Darfield, past fertile if muddy paddocks that accommodated rare combinations of ducks and sheep, the gravity inside our carriage developed a life of its own. Coffee sloshed uncontrollably as the G-forces bent us to their will. The woman opposite us produced a box of tissues and a goodly swathe of these served to confine the spillage.

Eventually, the train ceased bucking and the attendant was only too happy to provide us with further lashings and apologies.

So far, such train staff had been unreservedly generous and even-handed. I was reminded of the time thirty years earlier when we travelled for the first time on the old Vulcan railcar from Alexandra to Dunedin. We stayed overnight in a grey stone guesthouse, sharing the warmth and breakfast mince with several other guests, one of whom was the guard of the early morning railcar. He was a jovial, ruddy-faced sort and we were soon on first name terms. We shared a taxi — and the fare — to Alexandra station, chortling and shivering most of the way as the prospect of a jolly tootle down the hallowed central line beckoned.

As the Vulcan pulled out in the pre-dawn gloom, the guard — Bob — wandered through the carriage, his cheerful, open manner transformed to that of archetypical NZR guard-gruffness.

'All tickets please,' he pronounced solemnly when entering the swaying railcar. (We were the only passengers.) We thought he was having us on and laughed appropriately. There was never any suggestion that we wouldn't relinquish our tickets. As we handed them over to the now officious official, even the good-natured ruddiness had gone from his cheeks. Was this the same man with whom we had shared digs, mince and a taxi? Was this his little brush with power? Mind you, this was in the days before 'have a nice day' tokenism and other equally shallow responses. I suppose you could say that at least you knew where you stood, and could stand. (This included not standing in the vestibule even if you were merely waiting to use the iced-up latrines.)

The attendant on the TranzAlpine in 1997 would never pull such a dirty double-cross. He remained unswervingly affable even when an English tourist, a spikey little man with a wispy salt-and-pepper moustache, complained bitterly about the coffee spillage. Thank God Basil Fawlty wasn't tending him. The wispy moustache might have found himself bustled into the vestibule and elbowed from the speeding train.

At Springfield station the rapid exchange of passengers was unexpected. Springfield. That was where another rail adventure, or misadventure, from thirty years ago had reached its horrible impasse. On another railcar journey, ostensibly from Christchurch to Greymouth, everything came to a grinding halt at Springfield when it was discovered that ten days of continuous rain on the West Coast had produced a massive slip at Otira, thereby closing the line. Our disappointment was profound as we were virtually ordered to vacate the railcar before being herded into a mundane Road Services bus for the long, boring haul over the Lewis Pass to the north.

Not this time, though. As misty squalls continued to drift in from the south, the TranzAlpine made ready to ease away from Springfield, hell-bent on attacking the climb into the foothills. By now we had become familiar with Tranz Scenic's policy of allowing passengers fifty seconds to re-board the train after the first whistle blast had sounded. Economies of time-bytes? Why not the full minute? What's ten seconds between friends — or between urinal and vestibule? One or two backpackers sprinted out of the mist aware that time was standing still for them.

There is a touch of sadness too as we leave Springfield behind. Rosie the border collie is no longer around to wolf her railways pie on the platform, a heart-warming ritual that became a tourist attraction in its own right. Rosie died a few months back and no one knew quite what to do with their grief. Animals and kids. I recalled the Carpenters' song 'Bless the Beasts and the Children' and the line that goes, 'For in this world they have no choice'. Yet Rosie the dog was able to differentiate between the freight and passenger trains that passed through Springfield. She was able to make a choice. The passenger trains had people on them — and pies. Five thousand of the latter, if you take into account the number of years she had been meeting the TranzAlpine and its earlier equivalents.

We climb into the foothills and soon the Waimakariri Gorge swallows us. The open-air observation car becomes a Mecca for photographers. At this point we deepen our acquaintance with the American who had earlier described the TranzAlpine as a 'biggy', not that you can hear much on the viewing platform with the booming alpine air seeking out every hole in your teeth and every hardening artery. Russ, rising to the occasion, displays an emerging intrepidity with his camera, staying longer than most to take in the immediate grandeur of the gorge.

That's what the TranzAlpine is all about. Immediacy. No steady, day-long build-up to the main course. No barely perceptible climb as an entree. Suddenly the Torlesse Range is upon you. The deepening gorge is in your face. Cameras flash as the Broken River viaduct carries us into virtual mid-air. Dustings of snow have become drifts. We are now in alpine country.

Something like sixteen tunnels are negotiated, causing Russ to curse openly as the temporary darkness stymies potential panoramas of the five large viaducts twisting away as we curve towards higher ground. At Staircase Creek, the highest of the viaducts just about induces vertigo to go with the hypothermia. It is virtually a real roller-coaster ride, only the earth undulates, not you.

I repair to the warmth of the carriage, leaving Russ to the elements, his head stuck in the cloudy mist that flits down to add an ethereal quality. It's time for a pie anyway and in the buffet 'Biggy', the American, and I chew the fat and munch the pie. (Pies always taste better on trains — something to do with their glutinous mass being better distributed by the forces of forward momentum and lateral sway.)

Biggy has an interesting recent history. He's been travelling the world by train for the past six months although his father didn't bequeath him an oil well or a fast-food chain. In fact, he's been doing it rough in some sectors. His budget's as tight as a whitebait, some of which he hopes to sample once we hit the West Coast.

'Don't hold your breath,' I advise, aware of the vagaries of the whitebait supply.

'I'll catch some of the little devils myself,' he assured. 'Long as I can get hold of a small enough net.'

'Perhaps a microscopic hook.' Biggy grunted, getting the old joke but not liking it much.

'When I was travelling through Alaska I had to live off the land a bit, between trains. I made like a grizzly bear, scooping sockeye out of a river just north of Anchorage. Couldn't even afford a bed for the night. Then this old tramp who used to jump freight trains in best Woody Guthrie style taught me a trick or two. Go into town, he reckoned, and find a furniture shop with beds on display. Slip under the covers just before closing time and with any luck the shopkeeper won't notice you. A good night's sleep is assured. The old tramp reckoned he'd done that on several occasions, including the time he ended up locked in the shop window unit, doused with bright display lights. He had to endure the taunts and stares of street-dwellers as he tried to snuggle down for the night.'

'Did you try that method?'

'No. I got half-drowned in the Anchorage River and spent two nights in the local hospital. I caught up on sleep that way.'

It was easier to believe that Russ could be a candidate for a hypothermia ward as he joined us in the buffet. In his intrepidity he had allowed his face to become a blue mask. He was probably also suffering from a touch of oxygen deprivation. I could relate to his plight. His lips and tongue had lost the power of suggestion too, and I had to order a hot pie and hotter coffee to begin the thawing out process.

'Can get nippy out there if you're not used to it,' the attendant smirked.

'Right,' Russ mumbled. It was a relief to know that he had retained the power of speech, although it was just the one word so far.

'Got some great shots,' he continued between slurps of coffee.

We returned to our seats as the train plied the ever-widening upper reaches of the Waimakariri. The man with the broken arms appeared to be meeting the challenge of ingesting club sandwiches with his feet, until we realised his companion had somehow inserted her right arm into the equation.

Across the aisle a couple of Marlborough businessmen and their wives were livening up, inspired as much by the scenery as they were by cans of Steinlager. Prompted, perhaps, by the plight of the man with the broken arms, one of the Marlborians was telling a terrible joke about the guy with no arms or legs who went courting a woman who had advertised for a male companion. From his wheelchair the guy had rung the doorbell and announced that despite his handicap he was more than capable of fulfilling her desires.

'How do I know that?' the woman asked.

'Well, I didn't ring the doorbell with my nose,' was the reply.

A good deal of snorting ensued as the yarn spun around. Outside, the countryside had assumed the colour of suede leather.

'This is real tiger country, mate. We came through here last Christmas. Talk about blowflies, like Coober Pedy on a bad day.'

Across the Waimakariri, a lodge nestling on the far bank was pointed out to us by the PA announcer. University students use the lodge while learning aspects of alpine flora and fauna — and birds and bees. One of the Marlborians roared.

'You hear that? Birds and bees. Students, eh? What a dag.'

In the same area some quick-witted entrepreneur had convinced his lodge guests that just beyond the braided reaches, about a mile back into the tussock, there was solid evidence of a moa colony. Such a disclosure reached the local press, engendering much speculation about alleged moa sightings. Expert opinion was sought and soon concluded that the chances of moa being found were about as likely as Buller winning the Ranfurly Shield. But then no one had predicted the discovery of the allegedly extinct notornis several years ago. And who would have picked Marlborough to win the Ranfurly Shield in 1973?

Such musings are put to one side as the TranzAlpine glides into Arthur's Pass, nestled in the middle of the Main Divide. Or is it the Great Divide? It's a pity we're not in the company of Australians, some of whom like to get the drop on New Zealanders. If Australians find a moderate undulation on their marsupial-pocked plains they are inclined to call such mounds the Great Divide. This would silence most plain-dwelling Aussies, although the talk would soon turn to the lack of deserts in New Zealand.

Arthur's Pass station was decidedly alpine. We could have been transplanted to the Innsbruck hinterland, or Lake Louise in the heart of the Canadian Rockies. The communality of train travel was affirmed at Arthur's Pass, when a complete stranger took our photos, set against the Tranz Scenic logo on our carriage and the towering mountain behind us. Up here in the Pass the swirling mists and flurries had disappeared. Were we above all that, above the clouds in fact?

On the platform, passengers swirled. Snow deposits mottled the asphalt. Suddenly a small green bird stalked purposefully out of the shadows.

'Look, a kiwi,' a young Japanese girl exclaimed.

I laughed condescendingly before suggesting it was a weka.

'It's a kea, you dork,' Russ interjected somewhat harshly.

It was, too, although the Japanese girl thought it might be a bird called a dork. The kea's infamous curved beak was now coming into focus, the same beak that strips the rubber lining off car windows and electrical insulators. And carriage windows?

Russ, inspired by the spontaneous guest appearance of the kea (had it been released by Tranz Scenic officials, aware that with the sad demise of Springfield's Rosie, a new legend needed to be honed?), revealed his most dramatic paparazzi stance. The idea was to shoot the kea against the carriage, with the Tranz Scenic logo clearly visible in the background. To achieve this, Russ was obliged to stoop and kneel, droop and finally drop into a fully prone position on the platform. The photo was finally taken with Russ lying on his back across a snow drift, his duffel coat riding up around his armpits.

'Ah, dlunk,' a group of Japanese observed, most of whom began lining Russ up with their camcorders and telephoto lenses. You had to admire his professionalism. That bystanders might consider Russ a collapsed drunkard concerned him less than capturing 'Keith the kea' (the sobriquet was coined some time later) in the best possible aspect. You suspected at that point that he would virtually lie down on the tracks if the outcome was a moving shot of the slowly departing TranzAlpine.

Russ had also made the acquaintance of a Japanese woman who placed train staff on the same pedestal as pop stars. She had an autograph book full of the names of guards, attendants and drivers from the many trains she had travelled on. She would add the autograph of the TranzAlpine driver before we Arthur's Pass.

All the rain-drenched beauty of the West Coast lies before us as we thunder out of the Otira Tunnel. Nothing for it really, but to soak up the sights and disappear into a trance for an hour or so, until the TranzAlpine glides importantly into Greymouth station. The train is greeted jovially, like a lifeline from the outside world. In the old days the arrival of precious survival provisions would have set the town folk aglow. In 1997 it is the influx of people, however transitory, and pockets lined with plastic. And considerable spare change.

The last time I saw Greymouth, the Grey River was in full flood. Since then there have been several serious inundations of the commercial area. Now, after an extensive flood protection scheme, you can hardly see the Grey at all.

Our short stay in Greymouth was mad-cap. Options were limited, given the fact that we only had an hour to play with before the returning TranzAlpine pulled out. The midwinter sun was dazzling, the West Coast sky cloudless. A strong wind blew over the bar of the Grey, driving us into the first hotel bar we encountered.

Inside, the bright sun struggled through tightly drawn curtains. The taciturn barman offered little in the way of conversation.

'Get many off the train?'

'Sometimes.'

'Expect many today?'

'No.'

'Why not?'

'They'd be here by now.'

We didn't even finish our beer. Better to be bustling around the commercial heart of Greymouth than sequestered with some conversationally challenged beer puller who missed out on the last hospitality course run by the breweries.

The sun continued to half-blind as the wind half-chapped our lips. Was the brightness of the sun psychological? Had we been programmed by past West Coast encounters and tales of record rainfall to expect, at the very least, overcast skies and downcast faces? Here in the main street of Greymouth the locals were looking up, taking in the sun. Was this weather pattern something they were getting used to? The sun hovered, mesmerising everyone like stupefied bees.

'It was fifteen degrees yesterday,' the barman at the Revington's Hotel announced. Revington's. Now there was a real pub. Bitterly disappointed (even the bitter was sweet) by our earlier quest for the quintessential Greymouth watering hole, we had stumbled blindly around a corner and there it was. Revington's, where, if I remembered correctly, international rugby teams stayed. And dignitaries. Images of the '56 Boks surfaced. Jaap Bekker and Bertus van der Merwe waving to the crowds from the balcony. Did it ever have a balcony? And would it have supported Bekker and Bertus, whose combined weight would have challenged most West Coast viewing platforms? Revington's was tasteful and friendly.

'Off the train are you?' the young barman asked. A tall, bearded man in a pale-blue suit played pool by himself. Several tourists ate pies and checked watches. The TranzAlpine was due to depart in fifteen minutes. No sweat. One beer and a pie each and we'd have a casual down-wind saunter back to the station.

From past experience of West Coasters, I've found there is an incubation period in terms of familiarisation. They take a while to warm to you, if they warm at all. Braggarts and big winders don't stand much chance. They like their company down to earth. Men of few words. Certainly not race commentators sitting on bar stools.

Several years earlier we had travelled by railcar to Hokitika whereupon we entered a nearby pub for a beer. My travelling companion and I were both fairly reserved types, certainly rendered speechless by the scenic grandeur available from the window of the Christchurch–West Coast railcar and generally wearied by travel. The beer wasn't all that good but we drank it. Certainly didn't complain. After a while (about as long as the TranzAlpine sits at Greymouth Station) the locals began not so much talking to us, as including us in their conversations. We said we liked the West Coast and West Coasters, a bit like people from our home base in the King Country, we reckoned. Down to earth. Like a drop or two. Don't like grandstanders and limelighters.

The locals in the Hokitika pub warmed to us, two young North Islanders who had taken the trouble to come all the way down here by train, at a time when young blokes were generally hooning up Queen Street or bunking down in Bondi. We only had to buy one drink — the first. The beer began to taste a bit better. By ten o'clock we had almost become part of the social fabric of Hokitika, being invited to perform as travelling reserves for the pub's dart team, who were scheduled the following evening to play a match of some significance against Kumara Junction. That meant staying an extra unscheduled night in Hokitika.

And now, back in Revington's, August, 1997, just as things were thawing in the West Coast manner (we had, in fact, just been shouted free pints of Monteith's by the generous young barman), it became obvious that we had next to no time in which to down the frothy ale. After much slopping and coming up for air we bid farewell to the sanctuary of Revington's.

The equation would be tight in terms of reaching the train on time. Three hundred metres through the slow-moving lunchtime crowd. Three minutes, if that, to get from point A to B.

'Don't forget to mention us in the book,' the barman bellows as we make a dive for the door. Initially we are rooted to the spot. The dazzling sunlight befuddles as we stumble out of Revington's, with pints of Monteiths still in transit between gullet and gut. Like possums caught in the headlights of a car in the Awakino Gorge, we are drawn to the pulsating orb hovering above the millpond Tasman.

'The railway station's that way guys.' The barman corrects our east-west confusion and wishes us luck. It is now 2.24 p.m. and we have one minute to get from the pub to the station, where the returning TranzAlpine is poised to depart.

We break into a furious jog, side-stepping kids and dogs. Our legs are like lumps of lumber and we still don't seem to be making any discernible headway. I am already hatching contingency plans in my head. One momentary slowing of our stumbling plunge, perhaps by a brace of supermarket trolleys or a wedge of street-gossiping shop assistants, and the cause will be lost. I am about to suggest that Russ, being the fleeter of foot, go on without me.

'Leave me here,' I am going to gasp. 'Tell the guard we'll mention his name and include whatever he likes in the book. Bribe him somehow to hold the train.'

Eventually we reach the platform, dishevelled, two minutes late, flatulent, barely able to speak.

'No rush, chaps,' the train manager reassures. 'We're still waiting for a minibus of oldies.'

A two-hour turn-around at Greymouth would appear to have merit. It would enable travellers to get a handle on their handles, to set a spell. And it would allow for the 'West Coast factor', the hour or so it takes for locals to warm to outsiders.

Florid of face and foaming slightly at the mouth, we collapse back into our seats. Pleasant memories and pounding temples are further legacies of our furious flight from Revington's.

The return trip is, in some ways, even more majestic. I was hoping for a laid back, been-there-done-that sort of jaunt. Perhaps a nap or two. However, the TranzAlpine's not that sort of train. Although you return along the same tracks there are times when you could swear you've been switched to another line — something to do with the filtered afternoon light or the fact that South Island hills and mountains have two distinct sides. Bright sunlight throws the West Coast into sharp outline. The Grey River, often brown and turbulent, is even-flowing and blue-green. Beyond Stillwater, as the TranzAlpine arcs away from the river, glistening flax and ash-coloured willows stud the dark, still waters, the quiet recesses.

The patrons in our carriage seem different, too. Perhaps they are. Carriage D is suddenly an old folk's home. At least twenty elderly souls are rising to the occasion, spiked one would imagine by a round of bevies at some licensed restaurant in Greymouth.

Perhaps they descended on the Truculent Arms, the first pub we encountered.

The senior citizens certainly take centre stage as the TranzAlpine sets its course for home. Four silver-haired women are on their feet in the middle of the aisle, functioning as impromptu MCs.

'Are you all right, Ralph?' the one called Glad trills while sloshing chardonnay over some innocent by-sitter.

'Would one of you boys like a Werthers Original?'

The boys, average age 78, wouldn't.

'Edith is going to read out horoscopes, so watch out.'

In the midst of the prattle, a yankee doodle dandy named Herbie is invited to present a sort of Liberace patter. The mother figures around him coax out the lisping innuendo. One-liners based on body parts have the harridans clucking.

It is the hour of the senior citizen. At Kokiri another elderly man is highlighted waving something at the train. It could be a pound of pork sausages indicating that it is time he made lunch. This possible wake-up call factor provided by the train's passage is not pursued by the PA announcer.

We will soon pass through Inchbonnie, one of the intriguing names encountered along the TranzAlpine's route. I've always wondered about the name's meaning. Herbie knows. It is all about length, or a lack of it.

While this sort of talk holds sway, outside the scenery continues to throw up surprises. Tufts of bush at Kotuku resemble cowering marsupials. Natural hydroslides tumble from the vertically unchallenged cliff faces. Lake Brunner sparkles and the station at Moana, nestling like a houseboat at the water's edge, takes the prize as the most picturesque station in New Zealand.

Meanwhile, the 'Tipsy Games' continue. At an obscure siding, a forklift is seen to be either loading logs on to a wagon —

or taking them off. A jolly exercise in determining which is which ensues, a tightly tautological tirade in terms of the relevance of unloading as opposed to on-loading. Then there is a quiz based on aspects of Inchbonnie to determine various on-train lengths. Herbie handles this one. The chardonnay sloshes and sprays. The gentleman in a blue suit that is now splattered for a second time expresses displeasure.

'Don't worry, Edith. He's only a man.'

You have to wonder. The old spice girls are somebody's mothers and grannies. It's funny how, when you take exception to certain human behaviour, you tend to focus on dominant physical characteristics. With the old spice girls it is hair: candy-floss topknots that have been dyed, re-set, bobbed, bouffanted, crimped, crushed, dusted, permed, firmed, permeated with spray, hemmed, fringed, wet, set, let go, scalded, bald-layered, egg-laid, fly-blown. Hair that has lost its sincerity.

Through weight of numbers the women dominate their group. Seventeen fired-up grannies and a cowering clutch of old men; cringing, grimacing, blowing hard, looking skyward, sighing, crying inside, praying for peace.

No doubt someone complained, or perhaps the ring-leaders had slight 'turns'. Mercifully, the carriage soon returned to a normal level of conversation. Perhaps the sheer scenic beauty silenced even the most hardened harridan. It was at this stage, during the run up to Otira, that the phrase 'stultified by the grandeur' was coined. That's how we felt. This was no time to nap. The lowering sun was now casting oblique light on to the hill flanks, producing pastel shades and unique shadowy special effects.

The landscape became surreal, so much so that sensory overload and the power of suggestion took hold. Just this side of Otira the PA voice told us of a tragic landslide that had taken four lives back in some dim antiquity.

'If you look out to your right you will be able to see a small white cross halfway up the side of the hill. It marks the spot where the tragedy occurred.'

At the time we were looking out the left window at another scoured hillside and yes, there it was if you focused hard enough, just beyond that plug of scrubby tussock, a clearly discernible white cross. Russ took several photos of it before we realised that all the other passengers were concentrating their gaze out the other window. Perhaps there was another cross. Perhaps we had made a significant discovery. Photographic evidence would come into play, but somewhat predicably the photo didn't come out.

By now we were into ravine country. They get about four hours' sun a day up here, when it's not raining, and it is debatable if anyone's photo will come out. The ravine closed in as the Otira tunnel loomed. The large extractor fans used to expunge the 8.55-kilometre-long tunnel of diesel fumes were pointed out to us.

The tyranny of distance. Another phrase is coined as we head out from Arthur's Pass on the final leg. Travel weariness and homesickness impinge. Perhaps it's the sheer isolation of the Midland line route. You imagine being stranded up there in the tawny foothills. Just in back of Cora Lynn, Cass, Craigieburn, Staircase. Names that have a haunting relevance for these lonely reaches.

It is time to stretch our legs and earn our keep. As the light fades we catch up with one or two significant others on this remarkable train.

'Another day at the office, eh?' I venture as I introduce myself to the train attendant.

'You never get used to this,' Bob replies, casting a free hand over the lovely, lonely setting. 'Mind you, we've had our moments,' he continues. 'Once we made a special stop to let a couple of trampers off near the Bealey Bridge. They subsequently drowned while trying to cross the river.

'We've had a couple of scares with tour parties too. On one occasion a Japanese tourist managed to lock himself in the Springfield station toilets. So much so that the train pulled out without him. It took a fair bit of reconnoitring before he was able to rejoin proceedings.'

We are introduced to Bill ('Don't mention my name') Harvey, an on-board old-timer who was part of the action when the Bealey Viaduct was built. As a resident in the work camp housing those who erected the structure (in the time it takes a remit to pass through Parliament), he can remember one hundred men living in tents on the banks of the braided river. Two separate tents were set aside for married couples. One of these had a fence built around it. A chastity fence? Makes you wonder why the other married couples' tent wasn't afforded the same dignified protection.

It's all down hill from here and the lights of Sheffield, Darfield and Kirwee pop up on the plains. A perky, elderly Australian woman, certainly not one of the harridans, wanders past for a chat. She is staying with her sister Nora at Shirley. We do a double take. Surely Shirley couldn't be a town. Towns aren't named Shirley or Ron or Gladys (although we had recently encountered a Cora Lynn and a Cass).

'No, Shirley's a suburb of Christchurch,' the Australian woman reassured us.

'Well, that's all right then.' Better than Hoon Hay.

Dorothy, the Australian, used to be a bit of a hard case. In her earlier days she and her boyfriend Digger, at her own admission, used to 'peench things in Seedney'. Digger died in Parramatta gaol. She is scheduled to travel to Palmerston on the Southerner in a couple of days.

'Shouldn't that be on the Northerner?' Russ suggests.

'No. Palmerston North's in the South Island, mate.'

'Palmerston South, or rather just plain Palmerston, is in the South Island.'

'Don't forget the Southerner goes both north and south,' I add unhelpfully.

'So does the Northerner, mate.'

Dorothy realises someone is pulling her leg and punches Russ's arm, on the off-chance that he is the culprit.

'Perhaps they should rename the Northerner and the Southerner. Call them Shirley and Arthur or something. It might make getting to either of the Palmerstons a lot less confusing to Aussie travellers.'

'Well, they've done it with cars already. Look at the Nissan Cedric.'

'Cedric the Nissan.'

The TranzAlpine is slightly late getting back to Christchurch. Not by much though, about seven minutes. But the way we are rushed through the precincts of Addington station and into our waiting Range Rover, you would incline to the view that people have been waiting around for hours, unless our hosts imagine us to be celebrities who would appreciate some fancy footwork to unsettle the paparazzi.

By way of variation we are spending the night with one of Russ's extended family, rather than pitting ourselves against the cut-throat, level-playing field of inner-city budget accommodation. Whether we know it or not we have opted for life in the fast lane, Christchurch style. Our meal at KFC is not fast food, it is supersonic. Strenuous gobbling, no better than the gobblers we are ingesting, sees us in and out like battery chickens, in about the time it used to take for your fish and chips to be fired up.

After the time-blocking influences of the TranzAlpine, life in the fast food lane is sobering and largely indigestible.

Head south. That has always been a rallying call for New

TRANZALPINE

Zealanders wanting to escape the rat race and headless chicken syndrome. That's what we intend to do in the morning. Catch the Southerner and disappear into the vastness of the Canterbury Plains and beyond. Head south, in fact, on the Southerner, despite the fact that the Southerner also goes north. Just as the Northerner heads south.

The tyranny of widthlessness, that's what it is. The tyranny of being stranded in a country that is all north–south backbone.

You can't exactly go west, young man. If you do you're likely to be back by nightfall. Like travelling on the TranzAlpine Express from Christchurch to Greymouth and back.

Way Down West (On The TranzAlpine Express)

>We take the train
>And take what comes,
>So carry us oblivious
>Into oblivion.
>
>If Greymouth has gone
>And Stillwater moves
>The Tranz will get through,
>on diamond-bright grooves.

SOUTHERN EXPOSURE
THE SOUTHERNER

After the gloss of the TranzAlpine we sensed the Southerner would be more utilitarian, more old world New Zealand. Besides, the Southerner has been a going concern for many years now. But it's a formidable trip, taking the best part of nine hours between Christchurch and Invercargill. Only the Overlander of the daylight services takes longer.

We approach Addington station somewhat dourly, with a 'what more can you show me' insolence. We know of the long drag that lies ahead across the Canterbury Plains, a route with which we are both familiar. No pioneering push along virgin tracks for us. A certain flatness prevails as the Southerner pulls away from Addington and out on to the plains. Perhaps we now need mountains to give us highs and ravines to bring us to a position from which we can only go up.

The Southerner gathers speed through Templeton (closed any good mental hospitals recently?), Rolleston (opened any new prisons have we?), Burnham and its military camp (got any new wars then?). A sense of cynicism hangs over us. A round or two of complimentary coffee serves to clear bearish heads and by the time we cross the Selwyn River a modicum of positivity arises.

It was relaxing to travel over familiar tracks in a half-empty carriage. Because the train breezed along in a straight line, I would be able to scribble coherently in the gaps in my diary, something that hadn't really been possible until now. Or so I thought.

It was at this point that Phoebe, a young polytech student, entered our carriage and consciousness. Someone's daughter. Someone's sister. No one's fool. She crashed into the seat opposite us, laid her cards, including Visa, on the table, and completely transformed the way we perceived life, people and possibilities — at least for as long as she was on the Southerner, and that would be all the way to Palmerston.

I think Phoebe appealed so readily because of her unpretentiousness. You could also sense a vulnerability boarded over with humorous bravado. Trouble becoming an adult in a small South Island town like Ashburton, or Ash-Vegas, as she called it. Youth suicide started down here amongst the conservatism and hot, dry winds. On the flatness of the plains, within the unchallenged sameness of the mind's terrain. In the capital of 'kids seen and not heard' parental perceptions. Neither seen nor heard, perhaps. Nice kids caught up in the peer-group, mediocrity mind-set.

Phoebe's humour was infectious, mercurial. Irreverent but with a homely, South Island sense of ultimate decency. Nothing too far over the top, at least for the first fifty miles. The product, you imagined, of a warm, fondly remembered childhood. Growing up with snow on the foothills. Red-cheeked chases through tussock. The heartland certainty of '50s values. (Don't take your daughter to town, though.)

Phoebe spoke of days down by the stream eeling, attempting to finish off an eel with a screwdriver to the head, only to have the eel slither away, taking the screwdriver with it. Leading to the mutation known as the screwdriver-headed eel. Russ, warming to the theme, did a David Bellamy impression, pretending to dive into a swollen sewer in pursuit of the 'lesser snorkelled tuatara'.

Then someone came up with the 'plumed Pauanui power walkers', a privileged group of larger birds who strutted along the beach at sunset, bowling over kiddies and crushing sandcastles. Phoebe hadn't heard of Pauanui, the playground for the nouveau riche on the Coromandel coast. She'd heard of Caroline Bay, setting for some of her more steamy summertime memories. 'Lesser spotted hoons' hovering and 'long-backed surfies' waiting to take you for a ride.

The theme of bizarre, New Zealand bird-like mutations took on a life of its own, as the Southerner surged across the Rakaia River bridge, longest in the country. There was the South Island equivalent of the Australian kookaburra, the 'flightless chainsawer', a nasty number with black singlet-like feathers and viciously rotating beak; the 'partially-plumed shop-till-you-dropper', a highly-strung but pretty bird found flitting between lingerie emporiums and whiteware stores; the 'greater hook-billed hooker', a garrulous bird of all-black plumage, always squawking and questioning the referee's decision; the 'flightless feminazi', who prefers to take the train or travel on the back of large, lumbering, male mammals; the 'pied Taihape gumbooter', a pie-happy ingester of bad food and rubber insulation; the 'lesser deep south redneck', with Lion Brown feathers and a mean red streak down the back of a spineless body; the 'even lesser Parnell Peacock', a multi-coloured feather duster on shapely legs...'

Phoebe had to get to Palmerston. That was the truth of the matter. She would be meeting her mother in a light truck. Presumably the mother would be in a light truck, given that Phoebe was currently in a heavyish train. Phoebe's mother was a train buff. Had a nose for nostalgia. Rhapsodised about the wanderlust generated by the smell of diesel smoke. Became so enamoured of railways that the nicest possible thing her family could do to help celebrate her fiftieth birthday was buy her a real train. This presented problems of course, so instead they hired the Kingston Flyer, complete with driver Russell Glendinning, and went to Fairlight for a picnic.

The Southerner eased past Caroline Bay on its way through Timaru.

'Caroline Bay. Nice girl. Any relation to Clifford?' My comment elicited little response. We'd been laughing so hard that I think at that point we'd run out of guffaws. I must admit, my observation was a bit obscure.

The group of elderly women who caught the train at Timaru were pure, pleasant South Island. No wonder they call one place Pleasant Point. Perhaps the gaggle in the seat behind us were from Pleasant Point. They talked of homely things. Strictly localised. Local anaesthetics as Phoebe had it. Paralysing? Maybe, if that's all they talked about.

'I know, I know,' they emphasised to one another. Renwick Spleen's mother had had her operation, with a general anaesthetic. But there were complications.

'I know, I know.'

Meanwhile the Southerner pulled into Oamaru with its stately grey stone buildings and friendly waving people. Behind us the reverend Godspeed had passed on.

'I know, I know.'

We told Phoebe about the song featured on the TranzAlpine, how they played it on the PA system and announced that cassette copies were available from the buffet. Edible cassettes? Something to balance the perpetual pies. We did an improvised version of the ditty, applying our best nasal, West Coast twang.

> You look out the window, you look out the door.
> You look out the window, it's the same as before.

Phoebe was musical too. She played the guitar, oboe and violin. That set off another round of musings.

No fixed oboe.
Let the violin.

South of Oamaru we encountered settlements called Alma and Herbert. They sounded like an inseparable married couple.

'They've drifted apart,' Phoebe reckoned. 'About 50ks on the map.'

At one stage (the Southerner was belting through Hampden, although it could have been Herbert) we fashioned a three-way collaborative lyric, based on Amtrak Al's criticism of the lack of long-distance diners on New Zealand trains. Such phenomena are a feature of long-distance American trains, where passengers can revisit the romance of soup du jour, four courses, corsages, a robust sauvignon blanc to accompany the fish of the day, after-dinner mints, topped off by a blast of Napoleon brandy.

'You can still make it with the ladies on those long-distance diners, buddy,' I remember Al saying in a moment of political incorrectness. Couldn't really imagine Al, penguin-suited, making such a play. He'd be more like prat of the day. The discussion evoked memories of the old cad of the day and night persona of the golden age of American railroads, when the tall, dark and handsomes made their moves as the Pullman coaches converted into veritable moving motel roomettes.

Meanwhile, our three-way lyric, which started life as 'Long Distance Diner', had now become 'Long Distance Dinah'. The latter, according to our song, was a very American lady who went all the way. Christchurch to Invercargill, in fact, and then fooled everyone waiting for her favours, bluffed them moreover, by establishing some sort of connection to Bluff. Or was it the dining car — the diner — that got connected. Innuendo infused the song and the process of linking with the Bluff service took on a coital aspect. Aphrodisiac references were touched on too. The train diner/Dinah was coupling with a service known as the Oyster Catcher. Cads, prats and Napoleon brandies were left languishing.

I managed to scribble down the words to the song as the Southerner continued south beyond Shag Point.

> If things get rough at Bluff,
> We'll tough it out at Inver,
> And settle in the diner.
> She'll have us in for dinner.
>
> Nothing could be finer,
> than to share a pair of tiffs,
> with long-distance Dinah.

We started work on another piece called 'Home, Home on the Range Rover', but the serving of complimentary morning tea and Russ's desire to get some shots of the Moeraki boulders (we were already well past that point and besides, you couldn't see the boulders from the train) broke the flow, which had probably run its course anyway. But not before we pledged to do this again, with a view to cobbling together a collection of on-board poems, pieces and songs rejoicing in the title, *Trainspotting and Other Skin Diseases*.

We said goodbye to Phoebe at Palmerston. I swear her Lennonesque glasses were misted up as she climbed from the train. One of these years we'll probably see her again, fronting some one-off TV revue. A strong tinge of satire, a stabbing of sacred cows. Poking borax at the pigs who stayed too long at the establishment trough.

Losing Phoebe left us restless for a while. By way of compensation the Southerner began its absorbing course along the North Otago coast, around the hallowed headland of another era.

I've always considered the stretch of track from Oamaru south to be a revisiting of essential New Zealand European roots. Oamaru, a monument in stone, redolent of an unmoving, unmovable Scottish settlement, is as grey as oatmeal. Often as cold as cold porridge. Willow Glen, on the fringes of the town, is where Janet Frame grew up. The description in her autobiography of the train journey down the line to Dunedin encapsulated a time-frame and an essentially European vision of the landscape, both interior and exterior.

Despite the ravages of the 1980s and the hiccupping recovery of the late 1990s, the meandering trip along the Otago coast to Dunedin still seemed like something out of the 1950s. A time-warp where locals, even in this dislocated decade, still waved at passing trains.

Modest bungalows and cob cottages hug the hills overlooking the sea. Incredible views of the blue Pacific above Karitane and Blueskin Bay suddenly render the Southerner as scenic as anything Tranz Scenic can offer. Remnants of the past appear as well. Grim reminders on a perfect winter day. Seacliff, once a Gothic mental institution, is now indeed just a cliff. In the days when it used to brood above the breakers, Janet Frame paid the price for being different in an arch-conservative age, wasting precious time incarcerated. Cherry Farm, near Waikouiti, also once a mental institution, is now closed by the ideologues and number-crunchers of the Health Reform Army. At Waikouiti, long grass grows up through a deserted place of confinement and caring. Such relics of broken lives are strewn along this beautiful, rugged stretch of coast.

Where do they go, the people who used to seek solace in such places? There is a profound sense of New Zealand's angst-ridden European psyche as the Southerner climbs around the headlands leading to Dunedin. As the train climbs beyond Careys Bay and Port Chalmers, you look towards the Otago Harbour entrance, on the fringe of which the damned hamlet of Aramoana sits in isolation.

The Aramoana massacre of 1990 came at a time when the institution-as-sanctuary concept was being debunked. You'd have to be a fool not to suspect some sort of connection between the lack of support for the David Grays of this world and the dreadful outpourings of violence and grief.

Janet Frame couldn't get out of an institution; David Gray, the Aramoana gunman, couldn't get into one. Dangerous extremes. The Southerner continues past Ravensbourne, virtually opposite Anderson's Bay. Somewhere up there is Every Street (there's something chillingly appropriate about the commonplace nature of the name) where the Bain murders reminded the nation of its dysfunctional '90s heritage. Looking across the causeway, you can picture Larnach Castle posing on the peninsula. And you're not surprised to learn that Larnach, of castle fame, came to a tragic end too.

Is it the weather, often dour, cold and relentless? Has it been the harsh Calvinistic attitude to life? A lack of true compassion transported from the wastelands of Scotland, where scrag ends and pure survival seemed to be the lot of the inhabitants. Tossing cabers in the mist and eating sheep entrails washed down with fiery whisky that left you hungover and out of sorts. And all that bland oatmeal, as off-white as pasty features in the pallid highland half-light.

Such conjecture and morbid musings are triggered by a deep-seated suspicion that Dunedin and the Otago hinterland could well be my spiritual touchstone. My Scottish heritage awaits analysis, but from the first time I travelled on the Southerner to visit Dunedin, with its friendly, often freckled people, where redheads and beards are thick on the ground, where a love of literature and poetry abounds in the steep streets and restored villas, I felt a strange bond with this part of New Zealand.

The Southerner leaves Dunedin station and snakes through the southern Dunedin suburbs. Past Carisbrook, where the hallowed turf evokes memories of famous test matches and infamous scarfie escapades. The past is all around you. The old houses and clusters of ribboned shops and pubs. Real communities, at least to outward appearances. The suburbs recede and the train gathers speed across the edges of the Taieri Plains, over the Taieri River, around the rim of Lake Waihola. Clarendon, Milburn and Milton are negotiated as we forge ever southward.

Just as it was timely to encounter Phoebe, who helped us work through the monotony of the Canterbury Plains, so it was appropriate to fall into the company of a lively Canadian called Wade, as the Southerner wound its way through some ordinary country. Ordinary by comparison only. The rolling hills of South Otago and Southland are panoramic enough, but like all rail pilgrimages, there are bound to be bland stretches.

Wade told us his surname, but details like that are lost as the stories and revelations unfold. Surnames don't seem necessary on trains. Who gives a damn if you are a Zimmerman or a van der Merwe?

Wade would have been in his mid-forties. He had worked in rock bands in Canada at the time The Band was at its zenith. He knew Robbie Robertson and Levon Helm. Was devastated when Richard Manuel, The Band's pianist, took his own life. Wade still made his bread from music, but the heady days of the '70s were gone.

'You gotta have a gig,' Wade reckoned. That and regular session work. Wade had neither, but he would be 'pursuing certain developments' when he got back to Montreal.

'I wanna do a book too. Something autobiographical maybe.'

Between Balclutha and Gore, Wade put away four cans of Steinlager and the train manager began looking askance. But Wade seemed none the worse for it.

'Look man. A bit of booze enhances the moment. Always has. I've been riding these New Zealand trains for two weeks and I have to say there've been some absolutely far-out sights. I just wanna heighten that buzz. If the trip was flat and boring like going across the Gobi Desert, or dare I say it, the middle of Canada, I'd stick to coffee.'

'Like, I get off on the Northern Exposure trip. That's me. I really relate to those wilderness vibes. I can sense similar vibes in this part of the world. Southern Exposure, man. Like, you look at that out there. That's where the real people still live. Right?'

We were looking at the lights of Mataura, glimmering through the gloom, as the end of the island, and the end of the line, loomed. But why trains? Railways? Railroads? What was the appeal for a mothballed Canadian muso, travelling through New Zealand by train?

'The railroad's in my blood, and music. The first sounds I can remember were freight trains rumbling west or whichever way. Some of my early favourite songs related to the railroad. 'Freight Train' by Rusty Draper. 'Mystery Train' by Elvis. 'Last Train to San Fernando'. I'd forgotten all about that stuff until I heard some cat playing a version of a fairly obscure Dylan cut, 'It Takes a lot to Laugh, it Takes a Train to cry'. You know it?'

We did. That was one of my all-time Dylan anthems: 'Well I ride on a mail train babe, can't buy a thrill…'

The Canadian muso and I sang a bar or two as Russ arched sideways to get a shot of the event. Just north of Edendale and here are these two aging Dylan buffs harmonising, or thereabouts, on a song that could conceivably break down international barriers. Or start a war. The politico-musical barriers seemed pushed. My teenage daughters would have died of embarrassment.

The elderly woman who had been knitting since Mosgiel (appropriately, obviously) edged past us with a knowing grin. Did she recognise 'It Takes a lot to Laugh, it Takes a Train to Cry'? If she did she would have been a mere slip of a mother of teenage daughters when she first heard it.

'It's lovely to see young folk singing in public,' she trilled, as we swung due south after changing course at Gore.

'Kiwis don't sing much in public. In fact, I think it's an arrestable offence.'

'Nor do Canadians, come to think of it,' Wade replied.

'Do "Blowing in the Wind".'

A short, rather bloated Irishman, looking all the world like Van Morrison, had joined in.

'You want that electric or acoustic?' Wade countered.

'Steam-driven will be just fine.' The Irishman smiled enigmatically. Perhaps he was Van Morrison.

It was a thousand pities we didn't have a guitar. Wade had stashed his in the baggage car and was prepared to negotiate for its release. Meanwhile, Russ, who has a track record as a percussionist of sorts (I thought, how Southern Exposure is that, the photographer is both a philosopher and percussionist of sorts) was now thumping out a persuasive rhythm on the table top as Wade, the Irishman and I did a version of Dylan's classic, set against the syncopation of steel on steel and graunching carriages. The diesel engine's horn barked out a brief instrumental break as the Southerner breached the suburbs of Invercargill.

> How many roads must a man walk down?
> How many rails must a man travel down?

It would have been nice to have a female presence, to provide a Peter, Paul and Mary effect. Shame Phoebe got off at Palmerston.

SOUTHERNER

Somewhere along the line, just beyond the warm kitchen lights in those homely deep south bungalows, we almost got the three-part harmony right. It wasn't bad, as the train manager noted, while scooping up cans and generally indicating that the journey was soon to terminate.

'Lovely, boys,' the elderly lady ventured as she eased past us again on her way to the toilet, her knitting needles silent and several miniature bottles clinking on the carriage floor. A tipple or two had kept pace with knit one, purl two.

As the Southerner began to ease off, Wade got to the heart of his career frustration.

'I wrote a song called 'Terminal Junction'. Offered it to Gordon Lightfoot. He recorded a version apparently, but it never came out. Some problem with copyright.'

'"Terminal Junction". Isn't that a contradiction in terms?' Russ the photographer/philosopher/percussionist probed.

'Exactly,' barked Wade. 'You got it. In one, too. How can a terminal be a junction? Perhaps Gordon Lightfoot didn't get it. Perhaps he did — and got scared.'

The all-too-familiar swirl and fluster followed with passengers spilling out into the night at the end of the earth virtually, being riven by an icy blast off the Antarctic. We saw Wade shambling off into the shadows, guitar case in one hand, hand luggage in the other, a transitory soulmate now gone from our lives. We never considered for one moment that the guitar case might contain little more than dirty laundry. Van Morrison was locked in some administrative hassle over the release of a certain suitcase, and the little old Mosgiel knitter was engulfed by grandchildren, their cheeks reddening and breath vaporising as the temperatures dropped to minus something.

'Minus nought,' Russ reminded me, alluding to a TV

85

presenter's gaffe the night before in Christchurch, where we watched the weather forecast with a few misgivings.

'Minus nought.' Good name for a song. Or a TV series along the lines of 'Northern Exposure'.

We turned our collars to the cold and damp and went looking for digs, secure in the knowledge that we had entered an enchanted zone. The concluding point of the southernmost train journey in the world? The oldest train journey in New Zealand? There was nothing for it but to celebrate with a blast of Speights and fast gobble of KFC. But somehow down here even the fast food is slower than up north, the uniformed, young attendants with their Tanya and Natasha name-tags, less frenetic.

On a Wing Tip and a Prayer Time Out: Dunedin–Wellington

The returning Southerner hit Dunedin just before midday, giving us a much-needed half rest day (or half-day's rest). We wandered around in a bit of a daze, particularly after discovering that the grand old Dunedin railway station had been disembowelled to accommodate a Valentines Restaurant. Good to see the basic shell of the station still standing, though. Next time we're down this way there'll probably be a pizza emporium sarcophagus hiding any evidence of the stately station building. In the meantime, at least it wasn't quite McDonalds in the Starship Hospital, but it was enough to set you wandering. Aimlessly.

Dunedin is still a beautiful city, still screaming out for trains. The words of the woman on the cellphone, a local academic whose dream it is to make the Edinburgh of the south the rail excursion capital of New Zealand, kept echoing. The Taieri Gorge train already operates out of here, taking advantage of that stretch of the Central Otago line that no one could rend asunder. But there needs to be a daily to Palmerston, taking in the divergent coastal route past Port Chalmers, along the yawning cliffs above Blueskin Bay. Perhaps even as far as Oamaru. Time for a stout and oatmeal salad and a visit to Willow Glen before heading south. Call it the Janet Frame Express. Or Gothic Daylight.

HEARTLAND EXPRESS

After becoming disorientated in the Octagon and along several tentacles running off it, we retreated to a pub near Speights Brewery that had had the edges knocked off it.

'God. This could be Murupara,' Russ muttered.

'Feel the ambience, man. James K. and Denis Glover probably drank here.'

'More like Keith Murdoch and Kevin Skinner.'

The barman was an old-world, old-city mine host, one who didn't take your drink and throw it twirling through the murk before executing a one-handed catch behind his back, as a thousand lubricated X-generators bayed for something. This barman didn't wear a snakeskin top split to the waist, revealing twitching pecs. He was more representative of the traditional billowing white-shirt-and-grey-tie generation.

Suddenly my bearings came back to me as we mingled with the homely bunch of gummy chain smokers in the bar. Several years earlier I had been quartered in a motel just off Rattray Street, which climbed steeply past the nearby brewery. Cannongate. That was the name of the street, or locality.

'Cannongate. Is that a street or a gate?' Russ demanded as he thumbed through the Yellow Pages.

'More a cannon, really. I think. What I do know is that it takes a bit of abseiling to get there, but the views are suitably compensatory.'

Remarkably the motel was still there. They still had a phone number. Even the name hadn't changed. The Harbour View Motel. Dunedin's best kept secret. Somewhere to put your feet up and look down on the old New Zealand unfolding. The Dunedin marshalling yards angled away beyond the harbour rim. Thirty years ago the complex would have been blanketed in coal smoke as Js and JAs shunted their hearts out. It's quieter now.

That evening, after we'd had our fill of city lights, the TV beckoned. Because of our hard travelling we hadn't seen TV for several days. The six o'clock news seemed puerile. Prime Minister Jim Bolger making no comment about a New Zealand First coalition colleague who had or had not done something to incite a media frenzy.

The three channels available feature wall-to-wall B-grade police dramas. Dragnet drags right across the available band. Wild shoot-outs. Some woman PC police constable at the wheel requesting back-up. Some not so PC male in the passenger seat saying stuff that is marginally offensive. Several one-on-one stake-outs. 'Go ahead — make my lunch' sort of dialogue.

And the colours, or lack of them. Grey-brown basement surrounds, dirty black streets down which charcoal squad cars skid. Off-white underground carparks. And the complexions. Mid-winter oatmeal. Faces half-stubbled because of extended stake-outs, waiting for back-up that never comes. If it ever needed to.

Such TV fare makes for a good night's sleep and we awake to a crisp Dunedin morning. Our flight to Wellington shakes us out of any complacency. The comparison with train travel is marked. Brutal transit you could call it, as we are wedged into the 737 and told to buckle up and basically shut up. You get smiles and a shot at reading *Metro* before being presented with a platter of processed food that you have to eat with your elbows. Blue suits and crashing *Otago Daily Times* and *Dominion*s threaten to engulf you. More blonde smiles and 'Have a nice days' abound as you inch towards the exit, after the plane has landed on a wing tip and a prayer at Wellington.

'Have a nice day, Sir,' Russ is instructed.

'Actually, I have other plans,' he replies cryptically.

Then it is off to Wellington station to board the unit to Ngaio where we are scheduled to bunk down with friends. It's a bit dog-eat-dog as commuters swirl past. There's none of this 50 seconds' luxury granted by Tranz Scenic. More like five. This is Tranz Metro country. We crash into a Johnsonville-bound unit and are pleased to find the rear carriage largely devoid of Wellingtonians, despite the pin-striped hordes making a beeline for the leading carriages. We begin to feel a bit smug until a woman wearing what could be a beekeeper's suit, but which is probably the official garb of some obscure religious order, pokes her head in the door to share something with us. A vision?

'I would presume you chaps don't wish to spend the night in Wellington station.' A proposition? From a nun? No. It is simply her way of making us feel inadequate for boarding one of the carriages that have been disconnected from the train. Why, we don't know. They seem perfectly adequate carriages. Sheepishly we make another beeline towards the real train, hard on the heels of the beekeeper/sister of mercy, past the parted couplings that confirm her story.

After our reacquaintance with the rapid transit of air travel and our lousy attempts at being surburban commuters, the thought of travelling on tomorrow's Bay Express takes on a doubly inviting aspect.

WAY OUT EAST
THE BAY EXPRESS

Came down from the hills of Hawke's Bay.
Never realised a train came this way.
Got a ticket for the Blue Bay Express.
Made the train on time — more or less.

The Bay Express was no stranger to me. As recently as 1995 I had taken the long way home after visiting friends in Wellington: via Napier on the Bay Express, then across the belly of the North Island and through the heartland. Unfortunately, the day of the Bay Express back in 1995 came on wet and steamy, although the rugged scenery of the Kapiti Coast was on display before the banks of black cloud swept down off the Tararuas.

The novelty of suddenly heading inland away from Wellington Harbour and through the two long tunnels of the Tawa deviation boded well. In the good old days there would have been an earlier swing inland over the highway and on to the Ngaio suburban line, which used to masquerade as the earliest incarnation of the North Island Main Trunk.

The present main trunk link between Wellington and Palmerston North is familiar too. The Overlander on its way north plies the path before plunging into the rugged heart of the North

HEARTLAND EXPRESS

Island. Every station north of Wellington seems to start with the letter P. We're talking Porirua, Paremata, Plimmerton and Pukerua Bay. There's a song in this surely, for some folk purist with a love of trains, place names and the letter P.

Pukerua Bay, away to our left, has always appealed. I often chastise myself for not striking out and setting up camp in a place like Pukerua Bay. This is where a rugged New Zealand writer might dig in, within spitting distance of the capital, yet thrust out on some alienating promontory; the better to chip away at variations on the great isolationist New Zealand novel. Holed up in a weatherboard bungalow, the paint being stripped by the stinging southerlies. Taking walks along rock-strewn beaches, the squalls wrenching cobwebs from the creative brain, and with the regular passage of trains up on the cliff face providing an added attraction and tangible link to humanity, for a would-be wordsmith like me; a train buff afraid of total isolation.

Back in 1995 the rain really set in as we passed through Horowhenua and its population base comprising towns like Otaki (some group — it could have been the Fourmyula — did write a song called 'Otaki'), Manakau and Levin. Off to the west, another Horowhenua town, coastal Foxton, used to be served by a branchline, but that ceased operation many years ago. Great pity, really. It would have been a pleasant, communal way for Palmerstonians to get to the beach.

For some reason many New Zealanders chortle when mention of Palmerston North is made. 'Palmy' they call it, rather condescendingly. With the urbanisation of New Zealand, the focus shifted from small-town put-downs of places like Eketahuna and Taihape. Now Palmerston North sends certain eyes skyward at the mere mention of its name. Perhaps it's all about the perceived transplanted 'gumboot' culture that attached itself to smaller farming settlements in years gone by. After all, Massey University, mecca for bright young farmers, is an integral part of the city.

Perhaps it's the Milson deviation, the 'thumbing its nose' by-pass that now takes the main trunk around the outskirts. If the line still passed through the hub of the city, the developing sophistication of Palmerston North would be obvious.

And don't forget that Manawatu, the rugby province centred on Palmerston North, used to hold the Ranfurly Shield. That was away back in the mid-1970s, so Palmerston has already gone through that process of confirmation, when a provincial city throws off its small-town shackles and becomes the sophisticated purveyor of New Zealand's national sporting passion — rugby. Perhaps it was the losing of the Ranfurly Shield, in 1978, that kick-started the Palmy put-downs.

'It's not as bad as it used to be,' a Massey student in the seat next to me explained.

'It's a bit like the Hamilton factor. The cowtown down the line from big, bustling Auckland. Palmy, just up the line from the big, bustling seat of government.'

At least Palmerston North doesn't have that constant reminder of cow-town-heritage — the Waikato cow bell, hundreds of which clank incessantly in the streets of Hamilton when the Ranfurly Shield comes to town.

'Hamilton's got the river I suppose.' My comment seemed vague.

'Palmy's got the river too. And the gorge.'

He was referring to the magnificent Manawatu Gorge, eastern gateway or rather, cat door, to the city. The gorge cuts through the main dividing range no less, and has become a tourist attraction in its own right, particularly for travellers on the Bay Express. Some have already expressed a casual disinterest in the

Kapiti Coast and the hills and plains of Hawke's Bay. It's the gorge they want to see.

God only knows the difficulties engineers and construction workers overcame to thread the line through the narrow gorge. At times the train appears to be airborne above the Manawatu River, such is the dearth of space. Speleologists would enjoy this stretch of track. When the clouds fold down over the precipitous cliffs, it feels as if the train is plying some cavernous underground waterway.

Beyond the gorge the plains return, and the Bay Express pulls into Woodville Junction. At this point, in a very real sense, we have to go back to the beginning. Wellington station.

1995 becomes 1997. In the most dramatic announcement of our 'around New Zealand in eight days' junket, we are advised that the Bay Express is being diverted up through the Wairarapa. In 1997 we will not be taking the usual route via the Kapiti Coast, Palmy or the gorge. Instead, the line up through the Hutt Valley and Wairarapa will enable us to circumvent the problem of a derailment on the main trunk north of Wellington. The announcement is greeted with varying reactions.

Low-moaning passengers, hell-bent on seeing Kapiti Island and the Manawatu Gorge, sit flushed with disappointment. Others rather warm to the idea.

'Far out,' Russ announces. Never having been on the Wairarapa line, he begins loading his camera with a vengeance. As with a lot of secondary routes, I haven't taken the Wairarapa option since the mid-sixties. As memorable as that 1967 trip was, it is still the only time I've been on the line.

'We'll see the Rimutaka tunnel,' the woman behind us reassures her husband, who had been crestfallen at missing out on the Manawatu Gorge.

'Can't really see a tunnel,' the husband mumbles.

BAY EXPRESS

'But at least we'll go through it, Burt.'

The Overlander, due to depart Wellington at about the same time as the Bay Express, has been similarly disadvantaged by the derailment. There was nothing for it but to couple the two trains together, increase the motive power and take the detour as a single going concern. We christened the unique, unscheduled service the 'Wairarapan'. It sounded vaguely North American. Amtrak Al would have been proud of us. The composite train boasted a dozen carriages and many were the stares of suburbanites as this unusual service crawled up through the Hutt Valley an hour and a half behind schedule.

Train staff went into damage control. Cellphones came into their own. All passengers were given the opportunity of contacting waiting relatives, who would no doubt be disadvantaged at stations like Otaki and Levin, waiting for a train that was now travelling up the other side of the Tararuas. The new arrangement favoured some. One young girl's parents in Eketahuna were making preparations to drive to Woodville. Now they just needed to wait at the Eketahuna station for the Wairarapan. Those passengers due to disembark at Palmerston North were transferred to the Overlander section of the train. Once we hit Woodville the Overlander would be cast adrift to travel west through the gorge and Palmerston before striking out for Auckland. Perhaps the couple behind us could take that option.

One Japanese tourist was having a few problems explaining to his hosts on the cellphone that he would be arriving at Woodville from the south, not the west.

The train staff continue to work quickly and efficiently to minimise inconvenience and delay. Mind you, Woodville has its moments. An English woman becomes quite disorientated as the long-suffering train attendant explains that today's train is a one-off configuration brought about by unusual circumstances. She wants to get to Hastings but has already been told by alighting Overlander passengers that the train is going the other way, which is true, in respect of the Overlander. However, it takes a good five minutes for train staff to convince her that the train is in fact two services, one of which will go to Hastings, once the Bay Express is disconnected from the twelve-car hybrid straddling the Woodville platform.

Finally we head east into Hawke's Bay and the stunning rural landscapes, Colin McCahon country really, unfold. Okay, so they are just hills, but they have such a sculptured majesty to them. And no two hills are the same, as Wally from the Wairarapa sitting next to us, explains. Some are scalloped, some scoured, some outcropped or bejewelled with rock formations. Lunar-like in places and pared back towards the horizon like low plateaux in others. The spectral shades ranging through browns, greens and yellows are reminiscent of reaches of the TranzAlpine's path.

At Papatawa kids are playing rugby as the train brakes. A back-line movement is mounted with such dexterity that the length of the field is traversed, and we crane our necks to see the outcome. At the critical moment the train takes us out of visionary range and I guess we'll never know if that sandy-haired kid on the left wing made it to the corner for a try. A bigger rugby problem confronts us as we realise that because of the delays, we will not make it to Napier in time to see the live telecast of the Eden Park test between the Springboks and the All Blacks. The professor from Pretoria will be at the 'pork' no doubt, hunkering down in a corporate box to witness the 'taking aport' of the All Blacks.

Until now our passion for the game of rugby has been temporarily relegated by the lure of the railways. It says much for the magnificence of the Tranz Scenic system that missing the most important showcase of the rugby season does not reduce us to blind panic. Had we been on an old mixed goods cranking through the heartland, we would have taken the trouble to jump ship at some obscure hamlet and secure our positions in front of a public bar, Sky TV hook-up. The Bay Express takes your mind off such alternatives. Suddenly the showcase test match is only a game. There will be replays. Other games. But you don't get to travel through the sun-drenched Hawke's Bay in a state of wistful recollection every day.

Wally from the Wairarapa has shouted us a couple of Steinlagers to go with the brace of complimentary beers that mysteriously appeared on our table at a crucial stage of the journey. Wally, one of our benefactors, was more specifically from Southern Wairarapa.

'Lake Ferry. You know it? Not many people do. Pretty isolated. Rough as guts at times. Live virtually under the Rimutakas, overlooking the lake. Nice on a fine day. Good life under the circumstances. People who don't know the area — mates — used to laugh when I said that. A good life under the circumstances. They said I thought you said it was a good life under the Rimutakas, not the circumstances, like the circumstances was a mountain range. You know, like the Seaward Circumstances. A bit like the Seaward Kaikouras, you know?'

I nodded as the Bay Express rattled through Oringi, site of a historical development in modern rail operations. A milk train, no less, will soon be running from this point to a dairy factory near Hawera in Taranaki. What about a beer train from Mangatainoka, home of Tui Breweries, to Featherston, closest railhead to the Circumstances, Wally's stamping ground? Wally laughed at the suggestion. Absurd, he reckoned. He was a Lion Brown man. Tui was DB.

We soon passed Dannevirke, the Ormondville viaduct and village, with its faithfully restored railway station and bed and breakfast facilities. Waipukurau. The stately restored villas. The stateliness. In front of us the Hawke's Bay heat haze cloaked the hills, while off to the south, just beyond Waipukurau, an expanse of wetlands provided a contrast to rolling sheep country.

We are amazed at the Bay Express's ability to make up lost time, while not compromising passengers' comfort or safety in any way. It can't keep to its scheduled timetable obviously, but is doing its best to atone. Timetables are a timeless talking point. If you had removed the issue of timetables from discussions about good old NZ Rail, you probably wouldn't have a discussion any more. The lateness of trains. It was almost a philosophical issue. It became so entrenched in the New Zealand psyche that many travellers saw nothing wrong in arriving late at the station, secure in the knowledge that passenger trains almost never ran to schedule. Once, when a train did arrive on time and a group of passengers didn't, the latter felt justified in criticising NZ Rail for running trains that 'couldn't even be late on time'.

Not now though. The punctuality of passenger services is a critical issue with Tranz Scenic. The regular scheduled arrival time for the Bay Express is 1.22 p.m. It used to be 1.20 p.m. Two minutes don't seem all that significant, but the idea is consistent with the new concentration on getting it right time-wise.

As we pull to a stop at Hastings, Wally from Southern Wairarapa can be heard snoring loudly as the streaming sun spotlights him against the window. Russ and I, somewhat belatedly, mount a discussion on a perceived sleep-depriving phenomenon. Off the beaten track in cheap hotels and sisters-in-laws' bed-sits, nocturnal rumblings and mumblings have often punctuated attempts at sleep. Snoring was the problem. I should have remembered. Years ago as young students, Russ and I had shared a room in a Mt Eden boarding-house. Back then his pneumatic snoring and my minor insomnia were conflicting forces. In 1997, when the time came to commission a photographer/researcher for the Tranz Scenic scheme, I should have published an APB that read: 'Train buffs and non-snorers preferred. (Training will be given.)'

Russ gets his retaliation in first, accusing me of dropping large objects on the floor to disturb his sleep. I explain that my perceived need to cast coffee-table books, indeed coffee tables, in a noise-inducing fashion, is rooted in Russ's almost perverse snoring. It's like listening to coarse gravel in a concrete mixer. Like the sound of a back-firing Humber Snipe, slowed right down. Sharing a room with a snoring photographer can be hard going for an overstimulated wordsmith, his senses overloaded with the concentrated phenomena available on Tranz Scenic services.

In the end Russ accuses me of snoring. Like a grizzly bear with a deviated septum he reckons. In his defence he quotes a verse I penned many years ago, a throwaway verse that I'm surprised he even remembers:

> I snored last night
> or so they say,
> the walls were cracked at dawn
> And splinters from the windowsill
> were scattered on the lawn.

Napier station, set in the heart of the art-deco capital, is a whirlwind of activity. The returning Bay Express is obliged to leave almost immediately because of the delayed start. It's like an evacuation exercise or the good old days of refreshment room madness.

Wally from Southern Wairarapa sleeps through the pandemonium, unfazed and stressless. It's obviously a good life under the Circumstances, which is where Wally will soon be heading. Still don't know if he meant to get off at Napier.

TUNNEL VISION
THE KAIMAI EXPRESS

Tunnel vision fades,
All my hard dues are paid,
Tunnel vision dies,
Blinkers removed from my eyes.

The Kaimai Express sets out from a station that is dominated by sea and sunlight. Just off Tauranga's Strand the unpretentious platform holds portents for twenty or so fellow travellers. The high expectation of train travel is fostered by the very setting of the station.

The departure point for the Express is very much part of the city's activity. Not like some provincial cities — Palmerston North is a prime example — with the station and line performing the function of a coronary graft around the heart of the city.

On Tauranga station you watch the sun rise higher over the sea as our departure time nears. Seagulls squawk and swoop. Fishing boats swirl and eddy. Off to the northeast the port of Mount Maunganui hums with early-morning activity. The smell of strong coffee wafts up from the clutch of eateries clinging like barnacles to the sea frontage.

The night before, we checked out the surrounds of the Tauranga Harbour Bridge, an impressive structure which locals tend to take for granted. Great for fishing off and a handy, if illegal, means of short-cutting from the city to the headland. But the harbour rail bridge in all its arcing rusticity is one of Tauranga's best-kept secrets. Why the Kaimai Express doesn't begin and end its round trips in Mount Maunganui, thereby providing travellers with the experience of a train trip across Tauranga Harbour, is a mystery. Is it something to do with points problems at Te Maunga? Or marshalling limitations at the Mount itself?

From the platform, looking back towards the city, the distinctive outline and hue of the St Amand hotel and other architecturally challenged buildings from bygone eras, catch the eye — an older part of the commercial heart that thankfully has yet to feel the weight of the demolition ball. It looks like something out of a Humphrey Bogart movie, set in the Florida Keys.

The steady lap of the sea against seawall is complemented by a distant roar. The Kaimai Express, in the guise of a seconded Silver Fern railcar set, is approaching via the harbour bridge. Obviously it has been sequestered overnight at Mount Maunganui, which makes a lot of sense. The Strand Station is short on storage and marshalling facilities. It looks more like a suburban city station than a terminus.

That's part of its charm of course. Twenty passengers waiting to catch a train at such a modest starting point is alien to the usual departure protocol. The cavernous, big-city terminus tends to swallow you. Here, waiting at Tauranga station, there is a feeling of communality, as if all the passengers are from the same school or extended family, waiting in the bright sun to go on holiday together. Tauranga has always been something of a holiday destination anyway, but here we are in holiday mode, waiting to leave the seaside behind.

The English couple we met in a waterfront bar the previous day are taking the train too. We had struck up a conversation in Abbey Road, a Beatlesque off-main-street watering hole that featured Liverpudlian mop-top memorabilia and piped music that was almost wall-to-wall Beatles. Peter and Wendy were from Weston-super-Mare. They still sported conservative Beatle haircuts, circa 1964. Still affected Scouse accents, although their nasality could have been the effects of the residual head colds they still carried around with them. Inevitably we called the couple Peter Pan and Wendy, particularly as Peter carried his 50 years like a light, floating McCartney melody. He looked no more than 35. Wendy was more hard-bitten and the bags beneath her eyes resembled those of John Lennon after a hard millennium on acid. Mind you, Wendy was also a Rolling Stones fan, a dichotomous allegiance that inevitably hastens aging. Charlie Watts and Keith Richards are no Peter Pans.

From the window of Abbey Road the harbour and rail bridge provided a mesmerising backdrop.

'Pity the Beatles didn't do any train songs,' I mentioned obliquely.

'What about "One after 909?",' Peter replied.

'Wasn't that a bus? You know. 910. The bus after 909?'

'Who cares?'

At which point we explained the nature of our rail odyssey. How it was a labour of love, a passion, as was rock music. A desire to see the coming together of twin passions leading to the sort of conversation we were now mounting.

'Musical icons like Bob Dylan and James Taylor and Randy Newman managed to write celebratory train songs,' I continued. 'The Beatles never did.'

'You sure you're not freeloaders, buckshee trippers around New Zealand by train and all that?' Peter probed.

'Buckshee's an Indian word, isn't it?' Russ deflected.

Wendy was less confrontational. Not only did she know more about the Beatles music, but she admitted to a somewhat repressed love of trains.

'The thing is though, back home, trains don't have the magic of American railroads.'

'Too many of them,' I suggested.

'Not so much that as the fact that you're not on them long enough to allow the romance and wanderlust to set in.'

'No one's written a song about the Trans Siberian, mind.' It was Peter again, sounding suitably perverse.

'It's more about your class structure, isn't it? You know, the upper class not needing to use trains, the middle class travelling in splendid isolation in first-class compartments and the working classes herded together just behind the engine.'

'Not to mention soccer hooligans.' Russ was wandering into dicey territory.

'Oh please believe me, I'd hate to miss the train.' The Beatles line from 'I've Got a Feeling' came booming out of the speakers.

'There you go. The Beatles did sing about trains.' Peter seemed relieved, as if he had won the first round.

'Yeah, but not as such. There was no Lennon-McCartney classic called "Flying Scotsman Blues".'

'What about "Ticket to Ride"? Wasn't that based on trains?'

'Buses,' I affirmed.

'Day Tripper?'

'I would have accepted "Day train to Bognor". Something like that.'

'Meet me at Lime Street Station?' Wendy added.

'Now you're on to it.'

'Trouble is the Beatles travelled everywhere by van. "Sitting on a cornflake, waiting for the van to come".' Peter, lightening up, sang the zany line from 'I am the Walrus'.

The Beatle beat continued to mesmerise. The truth is we stayed overly long at the Abbey Road, debating connections between rock music and railways.

'The Beatles did a version of "Freight Train", you know.' I was stabbing in the dark now.

'Dylan did "Slow Train Coming".'

Somewhere along the line Peter and Wendy connected to the advantages of train travel. They had been scheduled to take the bus to Hamilton but now were pledging their intention to transfer to the Kaimai Express.

'It suddenly seems more relevant,' Wendy revealed, her Scouse accent returning.

'You won't regret it. You'll get to go through the Kaimai Tunnel.'

'Has anyone written a song about that?' Peter was on the attack again.

'It's 8.9 ks long,' I emphasised.

'One after 8.9 eh?'

'It's the longest tunnel in the southern hemisphere. If you go by road you'll go over the Kaimais and miss everything.'

'"The long and winding road." Yes, you're right. The Beatles were pro-road. Probably anti-train.'

'But buses are so boring. You're not even allowed to converse with the driver.'

'So you can converse with the driver of the Kaimai Express, then?'

'Probably not, but you can converse with fellow passengers.'

As the afternoon wore on, the intense relationship between rock music and railways was conceded, even if the Beatles never did do the great-train-rock standard.

'So we'll see you at the station tomorrow morning then?' I

asked as the piano chord at the end of 'A Day in the Life' faded.

'It'll be just like the Beatles at the beginning of *A Hard Day's Night* — the movie.'

Was that a 'yes' then?

'You know. The Beatles running down the platform to catch a getaway train.' It was a 'yes'.

'Hey, you're right. They sang "I Should Have Known Better" in the guard's van.' Russ was on to it now.

'There you go then.' And we did.

Now as Peter and Wendy made their way towards us, grinning foolishly as they stumbled on the buckled platform asphalt, it became apparent that a certain seediness had settled on them. The previous evening they had slipped back to Abbey Road to help prolong the magic of the Beatles revisited. At some stage a curious debate was entered into with an American rail enthusiast (could it have been Amtrak Al?) regarding the relative merits of the rolling stock of American systems compared with British. Wendy thought the discussion was about the Rolling Stones of Britain, not the rolling stock of America. It sounded awfully like Amtrak Al, although the bar had been particularly noisy with everyone diatribing over the hellish racket of 'Helter Skelter'.

As the Kaimai Express approached the platform Peter got the last blow in.

'Picture yourself on a train in a station,' he sang with the fractured tones of a man who had been chewing too much fat in a smoke-filled room for several hours.

The line from 'Lucy in the Sky with Diamonds', from Sergeant Pepper, the Beatles' most famous album, rather confirmed that the Beatles did pay homage to trains and railways.

'Picked up my bag, ran to the station. Railman said, you got the wrong location.' Peter sang that too, the chorus from 'One after 909', before being consumed by a coughing fit.

'Hard night's night, eh?' Russ observed, as the Kaimai Express coasted to a stop. There were no 'plasticine porters' with 'looking-glass ties' — just a friendly train attendant perusing our tickets as we took our seats.

It was good to see Peter and Wendy again, although they were reflective to say the least, as the Kaimai Express eased away from the Strand station, away from the Key West movie set. Peter wandered off a few times. Was he making contact with the driver in an attempt to converse? It has been said that some Englishmen can talk their way out of a paper bag. Or advance several sides of an argument at once. Peter of Weston-super-Mare fell into this category. He should have been (perhaps he was) a politician.

At the outset of the climb through suburban Tauranga we passed the main Tranz Rail building. It was here, after a sweltering walk, we secured our tickets to ride for the day tripper. Compared to the quaintness of the Strand station, it was decidedly corporate.

The line followed the harbour rim up through Omokoroa and soon views of Matakana Island and the Pacific Ocean beyond dominated the skyline. Beyond Apata we headed due west, hell-bent on seeking out the portals of the Kaimai Tunnel. There was no point pining for the good old days when the line used to continue north around the upper reaches of Tauranga Harbour before threading its way through the picturesque gorges of Athenree and Karangahake. It was more a matter of appreciating the time-saving features of the Kaimai Tunnel, a matter of understanding the herculean engineering feat that forced the breach in the first place.

The Kaimai Tunnel is the most recent invasive railway exercise in this country. In terms of New Zealand railway history it was almost an anachronism when it was built. In an era that had seen the contraction of rail services in general, the undertaking to construct the tunnel became something of a curiosity.

At a time when the motor car was on a roll, heads were turned by the quaint notion of digging a long hole beneath the very mountain that carried the new-age knights, speeding surfies and hoons unleashed in their four-wheeled chariots on tyres. It was, however, a freight-orientated exercise, a means to better expedite the primary products of the Waikato to the burgeoning port of Mount Maunganui. Significantly, at the time of its construction, improved passenger access was not a consideration. The old NZ Rail philosophy did not embrace the notion of human cargo. After the tunnel's opening a few excursion trains took advantage of the unique opportunities opened up by the tunnel's existence, but NZ Rail could see little value in reinstating passenger services between Auckland, the Waikato and the Bay of Plenty.

It was the longest tunnel in the southern hemisphere, yet somehow it could not be utilised to promote renewed passenger services. This could only happen in New Zealand. Eventually someone twigged to the potential. Now Tranz Scenic has developed the service: the Kaimai Express, a train title that took full advantage of the fact that the Kaimai Tunnel was not just any tunnel.

After climbing through the foothills, the train plunged into darkness. As our eyes adjusted to the artificial light, Peter and Wendy could be seen slumped in slumbering positions across the aisle. There was something very English about their snoring patterns. The vibrating stiff upper lips gave them away.

It's funny how you can make bad nationality calls in other areas, particularly in artificial light. The middle-aged woman sitting across from us had the countenance of an Eastern European. She could have been Polish or Ukrainian. Azerbaijani even. Her eyes were as dark as Poland's history, but they shone with a certain passion, staring into the middle distance, into some dimension a long way from eye contact. Her long, dark tresses were confined

— more restrained — by a severe headscarf, rather, one would assume, in the manner of the political regime she had now unshackled from her consciousness. And having done so, she travels the railways of the world, now that she can turn her back, bitterly, on the unmanned border stations, long rotting with contempt and boredom. Boredom at the border, and at the heart of the old Iron Curtain body politic.

She looked like a gipsy whose grandmother may have died in a death camp. Her lips, pursed into a disinterested smirk, had probably tasted deeply of the vicissitudes of life. She would probably fill a chapter of this book, but what could I possibly say to her to break the ice? In the end I didn't. Instead, I accidentally spilt apple-and-orange juice in her lap as the Kaimai Express jolted its way into the daylight beyond the western tunnel portal.

'I'm so sorry,' I burbled.

'Don't worry, mate,' she replied in a decidedly rural New Zealand twang.

She obviously wasn't from behind the Iron Curtain. More likely from behind some pohutukawa windbreak in the bountiful Bay of Plenty.

In fact, she was from Morrinsville, next stop down the line.

The fertile Waikato plains await as we head due west. Dairy farms sprinkle the landscape. Cows abound. Prosperity pokes through. Small settlements like Waharoa and Walton, with their high-tech dairy factories and agricultural service industries, stud the easy run across some of the most productive farm land in the world. School kids wait for school buses. Farmers wave at the train. It's hard to believe that, thanks to the Kaimai Tunnel, Tauranga is less than an hour behind us.

The Kaimai Express gathers speed as the occasional showers sweep down. The approaches to Morrinsville seem a little grubby somehow. Perhaps it's the unfair contrast with up-market areas of suburban Tauranga, our last point of built-up reference. Perhaps its the showery weather. Morrinsville station is functional enough — and significant. It is a fully-fledged passenger junction. Very few New Zealand country towns can lay similar claims. The Rotorua link, off-shoot for the Geyserland Express, branches off here. At least that's the way I remembered it. Morrinsville Junction used to be a busy interchange in days when steam passenger services were common. My father has a photograph of the station precincts taken in the late 1930s. Three express trains are exchanging passengers. One is the Taneatua Express heading east, another a Hamilton-bound service. The third is the once-famous Rotorua Express that enabled the well-heeled of Auckland to take the thermal waters and generally gambol around the steamy wonderland that was pre-World War II Rotorua.

While reminiscing about Morrinsville's history, and indeed current status as a passenger junction, we come to the conclusion that there is nothing to stop us leaving the Kaimai Express here, preparatory to connecting with the downward Geyserland, which shouldn't be too far back up the tracks. Our original intention was to connect with the Rotorua train at Hamilton. However, by the time we discuss logistics and minor violation of ticketing arrangements, the Kaimai Express battens down hatches and makes ready to depart.

It's still drizzling outside and the interior of the train remains warm and welcoming. Had we been a bit more intrepid we could have made a charge for the vestibule and braved the elements, such as they were. We have become rather smug and insulated. The Kaimai Express is not exactly the Patagonian Daylight with cages of live poultry and clumps of onions swinging from the baggage racks. Nor are there paunchy gauchos poised in the aisle to steal our seats. Besides, we've only been travelling for an hour.

'Waharoa's the junction now,' an elderly woman sitting across the aisle informs us.

'And none of the passenger trains stop there.' Suddenly the gaps in our railway route knowledge open up. It's not as if we couldn't catch the Geyserland at Morrinsville anyway. But it was an oversight on our part. And while Morrinsville retained its junction status it was not a passenger service junction. Not technically. Not any more. It would have been had the Thames branch retained a mixed goods or railcar link. But of course stretches of that branch had been ripped up, making it difficult for any kind of service to operate. It was all very confusing, and while the Kaimai Express sprinted off towards Hamilton we pored frantically over our relief maps.

There was no relief. A gaffe it was. A simple but potentially damaging oversight. The sort that railway purists like us shouldn't make. God, if this ever got back to headquarters. The new spur line that carried the Kaimai tunnel deviation to the Waikato network did indeed join up at Waharoa. Not Morrinsville. Mind you, the fact that the passenger service didn't stop at Waharoa meant that, logistically, Morrinsville was still the junction.

We reassured ourselves with wild postulations about how Waharoa should make more of the fact that it is, despite its comparative obscurity, a genuine passenger junction. A cashing in on the situation could be the making of the town. Something for an entrepreneur in conjunction with Tranz Scenic and the town fathers to work on.

The outskirts of Hamilton were upon us now. Ruakura Research Centre, the agricultural brains trust, the cutting edge of the local billion-dollar farming industry. Ruakura used to be a passenger junction too. Russ doesn't believe me, but an earnest scanning of the map reveals that the short Cambridge branch connects here. I recounted stories my father told of travelling from Matangi on the Cambridge line up to Ruakura, where he used to transfer to a Hamilton-bound train. That was how he used to get to school for a while.

The western suburbs of Hamilton build up and soon we are crossing the Waikato River, before disappearing into the tunnel beneath the commercial heart of the city. Trains no longer stop at the underground central city station. Street kids have won the battle with city fathers. Their lifestyle, centred on glue-sniffing, tagging, general vandalism and squatting, has made the underground stop an unsightly and potentially dangerous option. At least that's how the authorities see it. Yet I'm sure that passengers could tolerate the eyesore and possible inconvenience in exchange for easy access to central city accommodation. I mean, is it really Harlem or the Bronx right here in River City? If so, it is, following the picturesque crossing of the Waikato, a sudden and saddening indictment. Are we talking about shielding tourists from a harsh New Zealand reality? A pock mark on our clean, green image? Or is this administrative overreaction?

Such weighty suppositions dissolve as the Kaimai Express pulls into the angled platform at Hamilton station. It is time to de-train.

Peter and Wendy are still snoring through stiff upper lips. They are scheduled to spend the night with friends, physiotherapists both, in Remuera. They can afford to sleep through Remuera station. The Kaimai Express probably doesn't stop there anyway. Hamilton station, although only a stone's throw from our home base, could be a mosquito-ridden Alaskan junction. Or the terminus at Weston-super-Mare.

We are still a long way from home in every sense but the physical.

INTO THE STEAMY BEYOND THE GEYSERLAND

Shady rendezvous, shall we dance?
First G and T at Circumstance.

Remember the romance of the railways? Me neither. Not the way the old-world promotional posters used to portray it. The pre-war Rotorua Express used to have it, apparently, in days when romance could have been construed to include lingering stares or wicked sidelong glances, a sense of something half-forbidden, miles from home, with the social shackles easing. A hint of abandonment in confined spaces.

If that's what it was, did anything ever really happen? Was it merely wishful thinking between termini? Can't imagine our grandparents getting up to anything too risqué as the train climbed into the steamy beyond, towards thermal wonderlands where the waters were to be taken. Were they hinting at steamed up windows, and the last waltz in Waharoa? Last Tango in Tirau? If so, the steamed-up windows of romantic railways antiquity were probably the work of steam-heating systems, a by-product of the old steam-engine motive force. Any other trappings would be difficult to qualify. After all, the route was an open book. No tunnels in which to steal a kiss even.

But you never know. Things were always kept pretty much under wraps in those days. And trains have always had the potential to harbour certain illicit situations. Shady rendezvous, ships in the night, although the old Rotorua Express was a daytime fling.

You could say that much of the romance of the Rotorua link, if we're still talking basic Mills and Boon, has gone. These days the Rotorua-line incarnation, the Geyserland, is very much a tourist train. A jolly four-hour jaunt from Auckland to Rotorua along a stretch of track that hasn't seen passenger services for decades.

We prepare to board the Geyserland at Hamilton, the halfway mark, with the gracious assistance of a dapper Englishman who bears a striking resemblance to Michael Palin. He rather destroys the myth of the monosyllabic PA announcer, with saucy predictions about passengers taking advantage of on-board liquor services. The Kaimai Express, heading north, passes through some minutes before the Geyserland's arrival, and passengers are advised that they have the option of being 'quite nicely by Ngaruawahia' and 'high by Huntly', if that is their wont. Or, if you are going the other way on the Geyserland, 'merry by Morrinsville'. Rotten by Rotorua? It was a slice out of 'Oh Dr Beeching', as the station attendant orchestrated arrivals and departures. His large briar pipe, a constant presence, seemed more like a security blanket. He didn't really have time to puff, between PA announcements and multi-faceted station functions. Perhaps the pipe was a novelty cellphone.

We were obliged to wait for alighting passengers from Auckland to quit the Geyserland before we could take our seats. A phalanx of Japanese tourists filed off the train, so many that after a while we figured the same tourists were being funnelled back on to the Geyserland in a circuitous fashion.

Finally, Sue, the friendly hostess, waved us on to the train which, like the Kaimai Express, was a recommissioned pair of Silver Fern railcars. Nothing wrong with that of course. In fact, the Geyserland was tastefully presented, comfortable and hermetically sealed like all Tranz Scenic services. Little chance of steamed-up windows in this environment.

For someone travelling east from Hamilton for the first time the descent into the central city tunnel, Waikato's only underground railway, might come as something of a surprise. It must be breathtaking for a novice to emerge from the black hole and immediately scale the heights of the Waikato rail bridge while looking down on the deep green river far below.

The Waikato plains are brilliantly green at this time of year, but as we approach Morrinsville there are ranges of hills to the south that I didn't even realise were there, in the Kiwitahi and Richmond Downs regions — a bit of a no-man's land for me. Once again the alternative route taken by many railway lines opens up areas of our own back yard that have, until now, remained unconsidered and largely inaccessible.

It's haymaking time on the farm, and I'm reminded of the folk song 'Turn, Turn, Turn' as the hay is, in fact, turned in three paddocks beside the tracks. Large cornfields at Walton prosper in the sun, as the diversification of agriculture becomes apparent.

Just this side of Waharoa we see the Tauranga branch curving away towards the Kaimais, source of our confusion *vis-à-vis* the Morrinsville Junction fiasco. We are now on virgin track. From here to Rotorua we'll be travelling the line for the first time. Waharoa is a leafy village with the train travelling through the centre of town. The same configuration applies to Matamata, another tree-studded country centre dominated by uniformly neat homes and general tidiness. The train travels down a wide median strip between main roads, enabling the town to present its most flattering aspect to passengers.

You can look the place in the eye, unlike some towns where the train takes you through the scrag ends and back yards, or avoids the confines of the town altogether and carries you past industrial complexes, oxidation ponds and worse. Matamata looks prosperous. Horse studs stud the landscape and massive homesteads suggest a genteel life. The 'Home Kills' signs amidst the leafy gentility seem incongruous however. 'Plateau Honey' is more appropriate, although 'Memory Corner', featuring a large sign on a house frontage fence in the middle of nowhere, remains a mystery.

Tirau appears, and images of the romance of the railways resurface. The Okoroire hot springs are just down the road, where weekenders from the city used to hole up at the stately old Okoroire Hotel. Here the thermal waters could be soaked up, along with G and Ts and whatever else enhanced the moment. The romantic aspect of the Rotorua Express would come into sharper focus with such intermediate stops and dalliances. It was probably more a case of the romance of the places the train took you to, rather than a sense of romance inherent in the railway itself.

Putaruru, and we now enter forestry country. The dairy farms recede, to be replaced by vast expanses of pine plantation and lonely stretches punctuated by timber mills and yards. The 'Toot-n-whistle Stop', the current name give to Putaruru station, is proud to proclaim the fact that it is 513 feet above sea level. Which isn't too bad I guess. Probably a lot higher than many would imagine.

The Rotorua branch skews away further to the west beyond Putaruru. The line to Tokoroa and Kinleith can be seen carrying on due south. The line to nowhere really. Perhaps one day the powers that be will deem it desirable to continue the Kinleith branch south via Taupo, and from there further south again to a junction point with the North Island main trunk at Waiouru. The authorities would then have the option of running the Taupo Express. In light of the emerging reputation of Taupo — the 'convention' centre where convention flies out the window — such a service could signal the return of romance in its modern forms, to this stretch of track anyway.

The journey from Putaruru to Rotorua is a fascinating mix of exotic forests, merging into native bush as the Mamaku Ranges are crested. The line passes sawdust mountains and piles of wood shavings, a natural amphitheatre or two and unlikely clearings where hardy souls have planted hectares of maize in the wilderness. Despite the ruggedness and isolation, the line follows an essentially straight, uncomplicated course. A gentle climb beyond Pinedale takes the line through Ngatira and the milling town of Mamaku. Never been here before. I always knew there was some sort of settlement at Mamaku, but because the main highway by-passes this neck of the woods, I never knew the town was so substantial. Plenty of forestry-related buildings, but I counted at least two well-maintained churches of indeterminate denomination as well.

The highlight of the journey occurs when the Geyserland, easing itself down the steady gradient towards journey's end, emerges from the thick bush to reveal Lake Rotorua lying in the Rotorua basin. It is a dramatic approach to the city, wasted obviously on the clutch of Asian travellers who have been sound asleep since Matamata.

We pass beneath the main highway and skirt the lake's edge at Ngongotaha, before heading due south, past Fairy Springs and other tourist landmarks, until we come to an anti-climax. The stopping point for the service is a humble wooden station a fair distance from the city centre. I know it makes economic sense to terminate the train here, but it kills the 'romance'. Stifles the thrill of arriving at a bustling city terminus bristling with possibilities of one kind or another.

Yes, perhaps that's what the romance of the railways was all about. Arriving in the old fun city of Rotorua, with options on taking the thermal waters and meeting stimulating fellow tourists. American servicemen maybe, or members of the Auckland 'drinkies' set, in days when Rotorua was the place to be.

NIGHT TRAIN
THE NORTHERNER

Don't take this train for granted.
It only knows the night.
It tip-toes through the shadows,
on its way from dark to light.

Night train shuns the sun,
through the great unknown,
The heavens lie ablaze with stars,
the blessed day's undone.

Night train knows my name,
it calls me number one.
The heavens lie ablaze with stars,
the sacred night's begun.

Night trains have their own mystique and territory. To travel by night train is to enter a clandestine nether world of shadowy uncertainty. And yet there is often a sense of reassurance. Something warm and confining. Someone once likened travelling on a night train to being in prison — protected from outside forces as you travel through the temporary darkness in your life.

Night trains used to be part of our small-town, teenage experience; the thundering steam locos, blacker than the night. The eerie glow from the Hades firebox. Wan lighting in the carriage vestibules with moths and other nocturnal insects hovering.

When I was a really young kid with a fixation for trains, I was allowed to bunk down on my grandparents' sitting-room sofa, from which vantage point I spent the night primed and essentially sleepless. My grandparents' home was located close to the main trunk line in Te Kuiti and because of my obsession with trains, my parents saw such an occasional treat as good therapy — and a chance for them to get me out from under their feet. At that stage there were at least five overnight passenger services: the Auckland to Wellington Express and the Limited, their early morning equivalents going the other way, and a relief express or two. The sight and sound of those nocturnal ramblings filled me with awe, although sleep deprivation caught up with me once.

One Saturday night while sitting bolt upright on Nana's sofa, I caught a glimpse of an unscheduled, phantom, dervish of a train. A screaming apparition that obviously didn't stop at Te Kuiti. Unlike other night trains all the carriages were ablaze with lights and the three shrieking JA engines shrouded in flame. It may have been a dream. Or a delusion. I counted 27 carriages in all. Was it a troop train carrying doomed soldiers to their departure point at Queen's Wharf, Auckland, where they would disembark to some foreign war? In 1956 there was no global conflict. Or had war broken out under cover of darkness? My father suggested it might have been a test-match special, one of those swilleries on wheels that carried rugby fans from the heartland to Auckland for the big match. But this was late 1956. The Springboks had already been beaten. It probably was a dream. Or a delusion.

Fascination with night trains continued. The plaintive howl of the whistle, the distant hammering of pistons as the Expresses and Limiteds disappeared into the murky heartland with you, at last, a privileged passenger. South of Te Kuiti the hills closed in and population all but petered out. As farmers took to their beds and house lights were doused, an inky blackness settled over the landscape. In lonely, ice-bound hamlets, street lights flickered and station precincts pulsed. In your semi-comatose state you tried to keep tabs on the land. In the half-light, station names like Mangapehi and Raurimu gradually took shape. In this way you were able to be reassured that the night train wasn't transporting you to an unknown destination as some political exile or spiritual outcast. That's how disorienting and spooky night trains could be.

> This train is not returning,
> It only goes one way.
> It leaves behind it bridges burning,
> and loved ones at the break of day.

> This train is bound for somewhere,
> and has no time to lose.
> The passengers have paid their fare,
> and have no other line to choose.

I remember a woman travelling on the late Limited from Auckland to Wellington. She was due to alight miles down the line at Mangaweka. I had caught the train at Te Kuiti to the accompaniment of a carriage of snoring Aucklanders. It was already past midnight. After half an hour in the toasty warmth of our dormitory on wheels, I began to plunge through various levels of unconsciousness. The train shuddered to a halt at Mangapehi about twenty miles south of Te Kuiti. The woman in the seat opposite me leapt from a deep sleep into the fumbling reality of early morning.

'What station's this?' she whispers urgently.

'Mangapehi, by the look of it.' I too am coming up from some sleepy depth.

'Bloody hell. I have to get off here.' Whereupon a wild lunge at coats and baggage and a stumbling plunge for the exit sees the woman safely off the train. Gradually I focus on a piece of hand luggage the woman has left on the seat. Knowing that the Express would have little reason to dally at a remote settlement like Mangapehi, I gather up the bag and move purposefully down the aisle, barking my shins on hard leather shoes at the end of legs protruding into the aisle. At the same time I do a bit of barking of my own as I accidentally swipe a splayed leg. The subsequent low moan from that quarter confirms my suspicions, but there is no time to apologise. I make it to the carriage door and am about to hand over the offending article when I notice the destination name on the baggage label. Mangaweka. The guard is all set to let the woman go and reactivate his train. The woman, never having been to Mangaweka before — nor Mangapehi for that matter — has no familiar landmarks to guide her, not that you'd be able to see anything in the inky blackness. Mangapehi, a lonely whistlestop, has few landmarks as such.

'I think she needs to get off at Mangaweka not Mangapehi,' I yell at the guard, in days when fifteen-year-olds were not encouraged to raise their voices to authority figures. The guard grunts and reconfirms destination details with the woman, who is technically asleep on her feet. A good deal of huffing and puffing ensue as the woman and her baggage are bundled back into carriage E, non-smoking.

Within minutes she is snoring loudly and I am left adrift from sleep. As the miles grind away, I identify seven separate snorings. There may be more. I suspect some passengers are snoring in unison. One dishevelled heap behind me begins talking in his sleep as we approach Taumarunui. Something about 'All tickets, you bastards.' Perhaps it's the guard. You weren't allowed to use words like 'bastard' in everyday conversation back then and I prick up my ears, hoping to hear another of the forbidden 'B' words.

Then Taumarunui station is reached and all hell breaks loose. This is one of several refreshment stops, and snorers are suddenly transformed into human moths drawn to the bright lights of the cafeteria. The refreshment stop stampede developed its own mystique, so much so that its adrenalin-rush ruckus might appeal to modern bungy jumping generations. Perhaps Tranz Scenic could consider reintroducing the phenomenon on a trial basis.

This slice of New Zealand rail folklore no longer applies to the modern-day Northerner, the night train operated by Tranz Scenic in the 1990s. The Northerner is a far more sophisticated, sedate way to get from Wellington to Auckland and vice versa. It is a genuine night train in all other respects, though. The same bleak recesses of the heartland are negotiated with little but the engine's headlight to counter the dead of night.

I am travelling from Wellington to Auckland in the hope of experiencing some of the eerie yet exhilarating night-train sights and sounds. It is mid-winter, which makes the Northerner very much a night train. As we pull out of Wellington station at 7.45 p.m., it is already dark and the lights of the city trigger off a variety of conflicting emotions: wanderlust, homesickness, exhilaration and weariness. It has been a long day in the city and I feel my eyelids drooping even as the train negotiates the total darkness of the Tawa tunnels. Above the train, beyond Tawa, the suburban lights wink down from hillside suburbs. It is a cold, clear night and at times the lights seem to merge with the starry sky.

There is none of the pub-crawl-on-wheels aspect of early incarnations of this service: the nights when a jaunt on the Express or Limited invariably featured bygone sounds like the clinking of beer bottles and the chunking of guitars. Besides, the Northerner, New Zealand's only night train, does not serve spirituous liquor. The lights in our carriage go out early. Most passengers have had an equally long day it seems. I sneak off to the buffet car where a few night owls have gravitated.

Black coffee abounds. Some of the buffet dwellers seem to be defying the need to sleep. Perhaps they are getting off at intermediate stops and don't want to sleep through, although there is a wake up-call system in place on the train. Stubbled, sloe-eyed, some of the occupants seem to be appreciating the calming sway of the train and the dense black sacredness of the night.

I take a seat next to an angular-looking guy playing a card game that only seems to need three cards. Joe is an off-the-wall sort of wastrel, an English merchant seaman due to catch a ship in the morning.

'Why didn't you catch the Overlander?' I ask.

'What, and miss this?' Joe nods towards the flashing lights of a Levin level crossing and the street glow beyond. 'I work nights anyway. Always was a night person. Used to do clubs and truck stops back home. That was always night stuff. No, night trains suit me. Guess I'm nocturnal. Born at night. Probably die at night.'

'No booze on this train.'

'Suits me. I'm on the wagon.'

Palmerston North, 10 p.m. Until now it has been like sharing a stranger's living room. Waiting for the late news, playing three-card rummy, reading Paul Theroux like the long-haired guy sitting across the aisle. Waiting for someone to brew a cup of tea. Contemplating whether it's time to put the cat out.

Beyond Palmerston my second wind begins to deflate. One or two buffet-culture types fold their Sunday papers and slink off to attempt a spot of semi-horizontal sleep. I feel my eyelids drooping again. Joe, meanwhile is into a spiel on the lure of night trains, how they are an integral part of an increasingly nocturnal western world.

'Half the world works nights now, whether it's on the streets, on the road . . . '

'Are we talking night court?'

'That and everything else. You know they have night schools in Japan?'

'For those who slept in and missed out on day school?'

'No. For the same students. They just love cramming. Sleep sucks.'

Despite Joe's laid-back acceptance of the night, and most Northerner limitations, the guy who has been reading Paul Theroux is less enamoured. As he takes a seat opposite us, and cradles another cup of black coffee, we get the treatment.

'Can't drink on this train, mate.' He sounds Australian. 'Can't smoke on any trains anymore. Can't really do certain other things anymore either. Know what I mean? Remember those old-time overnight trains, mate?' He sounded more Auckland, actually. 'Remember the Express. You could express yourself on that. Auckland to Wellington and vice versa. More vice than versa. I remember once running into this bird in first class. We starting chatting between Taumarunui and National Park. She had this hip flask. The guard kept flashing his torch. All the other passengers told him to stick it. We weren't doing anything illegal, know what I mean?'

He sounded positively Ponsonby now.

'Something happened between Ohakune and Taihape. She reckoned Tangiwai could happen again at any time. Why not live for the moment? Seize the moment. I reckoned another Napier earthquake was due. You know, did the earth move, or what? We did a bit of seizing the moment, in between torch flashings, and finally woke up right between the two long Tawa tunnels. Just this side of the capital. It was a good night. She was great company. I used to be able to remember her name.'

It is time for sleep, although I know I'll probably thrash the night away. Always was a light sleeper. Perhaps I'm nocturnal.

Waiouru, 12.30 a.m., and I am sleeping like a baby. The result of having had no expectations of sleep I guess, together with that long day in Wellington. By the time I awake, remarkably refreshed, the Northerner is rattling through suburban Auckland, past the old Westfield Freezing Works. All the heartland haunts — Te Kuiti included — have flitted away on the wings of night, while I dreamed of greater Chicago and the North East corridor — and the State of Maine.

An early morning coffee is sought in the buffet. Joe is slumped in the corner of his seat, snoring like Russell Young, looking a bit like Keith Richards of the Rolling Stones. The long-haired guy is still reading Paul Theroux. He's more than two-thirds through the thick tome. Another fifty miles and he'd have it finished. If we had another fifty miles.

'Good morning,' I offered chirpily.

'Sleep well?' he replies, eventually.

'Great. Like a coffee?'

'Black thanks.'

As the Auckland skyline takes shape against a dull grey dawn, passengers mill about the buffet counter.

'Hello Graham.' The woman standing next to me catches me by surprise. There's a familiar look about her, a half-remembered smile.

'Isabel McCarthy,' she says, while extending a hand.

Isabel McCarthy from secondary school days. She's still poised and friendly, if that's the way I remember her. It's been twenty-five years. She's done something with her hair, but then who hasn't? The expressive hazel eyes are unsullied though.

We share a drink — black coffee — and in the seven minutes before the train enters the Auckland terminus, recollections of small-town life abound. Where are they now? Who did they marry? Why did they split? How are you keeping?

Isabel's in business in Wellington. She and a bunch of friends, capital city sophisticates by the look of them, are off to Waiheke Island to savour the ambience. I can't recall if we were ever that close at school. She was dux at one stage, out of my league at a time when rugby was my one true love.

Our encounter was reminiscent of the fleeting acquaintance we made with the English girl battling cancer. That's one downside of the rail experience. Touching base with someone at the end of a long journey. Despite the best will in the world and the fastest tongue in the west, you're not going to break much ice over the final ten miles. Last minute reunions can be cruel.

All bets are off, the interpersonal rules redrawn, as the Northerner pulls into Auckland. The real world is re-entered. Friends of the night, and morning, disperse in a frenzied round of slamming car doors and muffled PA announcements. Joe is at last stirring in his corner of the carriage. Paul Theroux has bolted.

The massive engine hums quietly at the head of the train, at peace with the world. I can't believe how fresh I feel. For once I'm not a casualty of the night train, although several bog-eyed survivors are grappling with heavy luggage and limbs that won't co-ordinate.

'Why don't you come to Waiheke with us? We could catch up on old times.' Isabel McCarthy catches me by surprise again. I've seen most of the great movie railway farewells involving parting lovers. Those celluloid melodramas featuring clinching, running, stumbling and wistful backward glances from departing trains. Obviously more subtle emotional business can be transacted on station platforms after the train has arrived. And a fair amount of wishful thinking.

I don't take too much convincing. Besides, I've never been to Waiheke Island before. One of Isabel's friends, a tall, young American, knows a lot about the Amtrak system. He'd stay with Amtrak Al a fair way into the argument. Apart from that point of reference, we are disappearing into a trainless void. One mantled by large black rain clouds and a certain uncertainty.

LAST TRAIN TO WAIHEKE
TIME OUT:
WAIHEKE ISLAND

Touching down at Kennedy Bay, the rain bucketed. Poor portents. Would we ever see the mainland again? The drive across the island to Onetangi was like travelling in a small plane through soupy, swirling clouds. We shared the narrow road with dungers and preserved relics like Humber Snipes. Red Ferraris were thin on the ground. The rain almost swamped us as we sprinted towards the only building that could be the local hotel.

'God, it looks like a bomb site,' someone yelled as we approached the old grey concrete structure. It wasn't quite what I had expected. 'One-hundred-year-old-pub' the travel brochure boasted. I had in mind a two-storeyed clapboard building set on piles perhaps, where the waters of the gulf could lap languidly and set a reflective rhythm.

The hotel door was locked. There was no sign of life. Had everyone retreated before an advancing army? Waiheke certainly felt like an island outpost at that stage. A last vestige of empire. Had we stormed the building just between the world wars? Would Humphrey Bogart be the only remaining guest, barricaded in the house bar, sucking his teeth and martinis? Mumbling about former glories.

The sky darkened further, highlighting the neon lights of an adjacent structure. 'The Onetangi Hotel', it flashed. Perhaps we had stormed the wrong building. We got wetter as we charged back through the monsoon into a gratefully accessible lounge bar. Everyone shook themselves like wet labradors on the sitting room carpet. Around us a handful of patrons stared out towards the crashing surf. With water running off my nose I approached the barman.

'Wet,' he offered.

'Wet,' I replied.

Next to me at the bar a Robert Mitchum look-alike jiggled his whiskey glass. Would Humphrey Bogart be along directly?

'We'd like to check into the hotel, mate. We have a booking.' I presumed this to be the case, as Isabel fumbled through her handbag for documentary evidence.

'There's no one up there at the moment,' the barman volunteered.

'Yes,' I said, not altogether helpfully.

'I'll be up there in about fifteen minutes, unless you want to wait for Tracey who should be up there in about twenty.'

It was the first of the delightfully convoluted Waiheke options and led to a considerable amount of haggling amongst our steaming and hungry party.

'Do you have a Trevor we could wait for, who may be available in about ten minutes?' I don't know who said that but it seemed a reasonable request.

'Look, I'll get André to unlock the place, if you don't mind waiting five minutes.'

Our travelling entourage, all seven of us, were invited to drip dry in front of one of those false fireplaces with fake embers, into which a nearby local flicked butts. Squalls continued to drive in from the north, and Onetangi

WAIHEKE ISLAND

Beach looked like the Gulf of Mexico playing host to Cyclone Trevor.

The juke box played James Taylor, 'Fire and Rain'. Was this Martha's Vineyard? Nantucket Island? Disorientation set in as the steam rose. The patrons in the bar covered a certain spectrum. Balding, bearded Jerry Garcias rubbed shoulders with spike-haired tarot card readers; vintners who spoke broken English shared a vintage moment or two with a lesbian couple.

The storm, if anything, increased in intensity. Some fool was trying to walk his dog along the beach front, but the poor mutt, a sort of hybrid Pekinese, was virtually airborne most of the time.

As we waited for André or Tracey or Trevor to unlock the century old accommodation wing, the lounge bar continued to throw up interesting anachronisms. A couple of David Bowie look-alikes (circa Aladin Sane) sipped Campari. A bare-midriffed young mother, her baby asleep on her back, danced with an imaginary, long-gone suitor, as the condensate oozed down the walls.

'House of the rising damp,' someone in our party mumbled. The locals were friendly though. Blair, who looked a bit like James Taylor, was a freelance beachcomber. What other kind is there? Does the Department of Conservation have executive beachcombers on its payroll? Chastity Belt, with her orange hair and personalised business cards, sold crystals, read palms, changed lives. She had a reason to be friendly. Business was not so good.

'You would have been able to foretell that economic trend,' Isabel observed kindly, the businesswoman creeping through.

Finally, the rain stopped and someone came along to escort us to the 'old hotel' whereupon we were ushered into the most time-warping hotel lounge this side of Blackpool, Waiheke. The precincts of the lounge and foyer should be preserved as a museum piece — perhaps as a museum in their own right. The mounted heads of dead animals, deer, elk and wild pigs mainly, glowered down from blistered walls. A stuffed groper, open-mouthed, served as an impromptu rubbish receptacle. An assortment of pre-war settees and armchairs circled the room. It could have been the day room in a psychiatric annex for troubled zoo-keepers. Or the smoking room of some Siberian hunting lodge, apart from the sea, that is. Paeans to tackiness, according to one of Isabel's friends, possessed of vegetarian leanings and animal rightist sympathies.

We sank into the settees, the poor suspension eliciting a chorus of twangs, and watched the clearing Onetangi skyline. If you look hard enough you might catch a glimpse of Chile. There was, after all, nothing much between us and the South American mainland, apart from several thousand miles of open ocean. The storm clouds dissolved and the sea glimmered. After the jostling of the night train and turbulent ferry crossing, it was deeply therapeutic to soak up the atmosphere of a bygone era. This was absolutely backwater with its own momentum and rhythms. We sank deeper into the settees as the sun sank somewhere behind us. You half expected to see steam train smoke drifts, and hear the muffled chuffing of a local stopping service. It would have fitted the time frame.

We soon learned it was pointless trying to hound the locals into mainland-like action. A young man in a beret eventually showed us to our rooms. We were the only guests. Had we been invited to a murder weekend? Was a movie being made? Were we the extras? Was that the real Robert Mitchum in the bar?

'The coffee machine doesn't seem to work,' the Tom Cruise look-alike with an earring and cellphone advised the young man in a beret.

'Barry will be up soon to have a look at it.'

Barry came up and had a look at the coffee machine, without actually touching or activating the recalcitrant appliance. Someone else, Garth perhaps, wandered in about twenty minutes later and after a bit of genial prodding which produced a magnificent blue flash, the coffee machine began gurgling. From that point on we realised we would be all right. The coffee, like that of the Northerner, was strong and sustaining, inducing us to make enquires about breakfast arrangements.

'The cook's away for a few days,' Garth said. 'Sometimes they leave stuff out though.'

We thanked Garth for this piece of information.

'Sometimes they leave stuff all,' the young American muttered.

In the quiet chambers of the hotel we slept deeply. I dreamed of Humphrey Bogart beachcombing in the moonlight, a stone's throw beyond the hotel.

'The lounge is full of hard hats,' Isabel revealed as we proceeded next morning towards a breakfast situation that was, at best, uncertain. A dozen construction workers had taken over the lounge where they ate great racks of toast and read *New Zealand Heralds*. A local arrangement? Were the construction workers about to level the hotel?

'No such luck,' drawled the cynic with the cellphone. The bright morning sun reflected off the hard hats as the animal heads surveyed the scene. They seemed to be smiling this morning.

We wandered into the kitchen. Someone may have left stuff out, although the construction workers had probably got down on it. To our surprise, a chef of sorts was in the throes of preparing a cooked breakfast, with lashings of stuff. The dining room was well appointed, with a continuing off-beat ambience. Paintings of animals in bizarre circumstances graced the walls. 'Still warthogs run deep' depicted a warthog running along the seabed.

As we walked away from the old hotel into the brilliant sunshine, it seemed as if we had been trapped in a time-warp for a month, not half a day and a night. The place was charming and bizarre, delightfully eccentric, a situation highlighted by the notice spotted on the front door as we closed it behind us. It provided information for tourists and locals regarding the availability of restaurant facilities:

RESTAURANT
Open Sat–Mon (except Sun).
Breakfast available in restaurant Mon, Tues, Wed.
Restaurant closed except for dinner Mon–Sat
(Thursday excluded).

Such perambulations were pure goonery.

'The timetable from hell,' Isabel reckoned. Still, as long as they sometimes left stuff out (Mon–Thurs–Sun), people wouldn't starve.

We left Waiheke moored in the gulf, its lights flickering, as the ferry gathered pace in the gloom. The red Ferrari may find its way to the island's shores one day and breed prolifically. Or it may be introduced, at which point Waiheke will lose its soul and people won't feel free to leave stuff out anymore.

Tomorrow morning I will be catching the Overlander back to the Waikato. Back to the end of the beginning of the round trip. Our utterly trainless dalliance on Waiheke Island — absolutely off the beaten track — had recharged my train travel batteries, at a time when the odyssey was all but completed.

But I had found an old friend, or rather rediscovered one I didn't realise I still had. And then there was Isabel and the capital city sophisticates.

> This train's a good friend,
> as old friends can be.
> Whistling a welcome
> It won't run out on me.